RETRO FONTS

GREGOR STAWINSKI

Retro Fonts

Join us on a typographical journey through time!

Fonts encode the Zeitgeist! But which font translates the swing of the sixties, the flower power of the seventies or the punk of the eighties into the language of today?

Gregor Stawinski has collected over 360 fonts from the last 100 years and organized them according to stylistic periods – in so doing he has been concerned not so much with art-historical accuracy as with a font's place in the collective consciousness. It is not so much the year in which a font was developed that is important, but rather the decade that it influenced, and clearly the two do not have to overlap: not every font is adopted as quickly and as widely as was Rotis in its own time (pp. 489 and 495).

Because the featured fonts exude the spirit of an era, we have called this book *Retro Fonts*, even if this designation is, strictly speaking, correct only for a certain number of the fonts in the book, which were purposefully created with a 'retro' look by the inspired collectors of type specimen books. In addition to these fonts, the book includes typefaces that have had a significant impact in their time: unforgotten classics and those warranting rediscovery. In order to present the widest possible range of fonts, we have also included idiosyncratic typefaces, whose forms may not be technically perfect but are chosen principally for their 'look.' Accordingly, Stawinski has compiled more than 500 pages of fictitious type specimen books of the decades, peppering them with historical and contemporary examples of their applications and, in this way, training your critical eye.

Wouldn't you like to try it yourself? A CD with 222 free fonts makes it possible. Fontshop and Co. wish you happy hunting with your new and improved eye for Linotype!

Wishing you lots of fun with 'type of the times'!

Karin and Bertram Schmidt-Friderichs

P.S. We would like to thank the foundries that allowed us to reproduce their fonts, as well as the designers who provided their work for the CD. Even free fonts have rules for use; please take note of possible restrictions on commercial use of the CD.

'This is your captain speaking': On Retro, Fonts and Retrofonts

Are Futura (p.196) and Helvetica (p.392) retro? Surely not! But, then again, is that really obvious? Whether a typeface is 'retro' is determined, first and foremost, by the context in which it is used. Even supposedly objective and unaffected typefaces may be used to surprising effect when properly embellished – for example, with certain colours and composition. Conversely, even kitsch and seemingly trendy alphabets can reveal, in the hands of a skilled designer, their modern qualities. Nevertheless, typographical time travel succeeds when, as in this book, the most popular typographical trends of different periods in high, low and mass culture are brought together in a vivid presentation. Only then will a review of the exciting history of typography in the 19th and 20th centuries provide thrilling discoveries, forge informative connections or simply entertain.

The examples of applications in this book show the context in which these typefaces have been set and how they are composed with respect to image, colour and form. On occasion they are clearly not set at all, but rather – as was the preference in the fifties – put to paper with spontaneous brushstrokes or practiced calligraphy. Among the punks of the eighties, for example, there were very few trained graphic artists painstakingly setting the type of their anarchic designs. These trends replicate the particular stylistic periods of their associated typefaces, and it is worth considering whether one should not pick up a pencil oneself instead of using a font.

Many of the fonts featured are available in several styles. Wherever possible, the styles are featured in the particular periods they influenced. However, all the fonts' styles come together on the enclosed CD, just waiting to be tried out in your own retro design – or any other design for that matter. As mentioned, there is a certain appeal in freshly interpreting typefaces outside of their historical context.

Before your journey begins, I would like to thank those who have helped me with the travel arrangements – first and foremost, of course, all the type designers who brought our extensive typographical heritage out of thick type specimen books and into the digital age, but especially those who permitted us to put their fonts on the CD. Thanks to the foundries and studios who made their creations available to us for the book.

Special thanks go to Thomas Heyl and Michael Keller, who patiently supported my research and out of whose archive so many of the historical images found their way and into this book. Thanks also to Brigitte Raab from Verlag Hermann Schmidt Mainz for coordinating this project. And, of course, I thank Karin and Bertram Schmidt-Friderichs, who made this project possible. Last, but certainly not least, I thank Joanna Krettek, who for years has lent her remarkable ear and critical voice to the idea for this book.

Gregor Stawinski

Contents

Linotype typesetting machine, 1870

1

Gründerzeit and Gold Rush Historicism

c. 1830–1900

In 1871, Germany emerged from the Franco-Prussian War as a military power. For the remainder of the 19th century, it experienced a new form of bourgeois self-consciousness. Steep reparation payments were flowing into the country, which conferred upon the German Reich an economic boom the likes of which it had never seen before. People surrounded themselves with rich decor and lavish ornamentation, emulating the lifestyle of the aristocracy and appropriating the styles of earlier eras from the Romantic to the Baroque. This historicizing style found its way into art and architecture, craft and fashion, and was reflected in typography as well.

MÜNCHEN.

Sonntag den 18. Jänner 1846

wird

Joseph Carl Stigler,

Professor der Tonkunst aus Wien,

Mitglied mehrerer philharmonischer Gesellschaften und Virtuose

auf dem Instrumente

POLYMELODICON,

oder dem neu verbesserten

Aeolodicon,

welches mit Tasten, wie ein Pianoforte, 6 Doppeloktaven und 20 Trompetenschallbechern versehen ist, die täuschend ein Orchester von Blechinstrumenten nachahmen, und zwar: decrescendo die Flöte, Clarinette, Hoboe, Horn, Fagot, und pianissimo die menschliche Stimme,

die Ehre haben, auf seiner Durchreise, wegen besonderer Veranlassung

um 12 Uhr Mittags

ein

CONCERT

im Saale des königl. Odeon

unter gefälliger Mitwirkung mehrerer geschätzten Künstler

zu geben.

PROGRAMM.

Erste Abtheilung.

1) a) **Cavatina** aus „***Robert der Teufel***,“ b) **Variationen** über ein Alpenlied ... vorgetr. auf dem Polymelodicon von dem Concertgeber.

2) **Die Feier der Tonkunst**, Gedicht von Langer, mit Begleitung des Polymelodicon, vorgetragen von ... Fräul. Denker.

3) **Des Hammerknechts Liebe**, Bass-Arie von Müller, gesungen von ... Herrn Hirsch.

4) ***Die Alpen-Unschuld***, Lied von Stigler, gesungen von ... Fräul. Zehetmaier.

5) **Damen-Potpourri**, arrangirt u. vorgetragen vom Concertgeber.

Zweite Abtheilung.

1) **Don Juan-Fantasie** für das Pianoforte, von Thalberg, vorgetragen von ... Herrn H. Schönchen.

2) ***Vocal-Quartett.***

3) a) „**Der Paperl u. die Nachtigall**“, b) „**S' Kristkindl**“, c) „**Der Baua u. sein Bua**“, Gedichte i. österreichischer Mundart nach Baron ***Klesheim***, von I. C. St.

4) ***Ouverture*** zu „**Wilhelm Tell**“, für das Instrument arrangirt.

*Eintritt-Billets zu **1 fl.** sind in den hiesigen Musikalienhandlungen und **Mittags** an der Kasse zu haben.*

Billets für Herren Studierende sind beim Hausmeister der kgl. Universität zu haben.

Prince Regent Theatre, Munich
Playbill, 1846

Gründerzeit and Gold Rush Historicism

c. 1830–1900

Thorne Shaded
Dieter Steffmann
2002 | page 18

Of special importance was the development of lithography, invented by Alois Senefelder in 1798. With the help of a smooth stone, it became possible to print freely, without being tied down to any particular tool. This newly-won freedom inspired creative, ornate alphabets and richly decorated pages that even traditional typesetters attempted to imitate using the means available to them. A preference was developed for using heavily-decorated forms of typefaces, embellished borders and lavish ornamentation, all of which were prefabricated as metal templates for just this purpose.

It was the age of the Industrial Revolution. Industry, urban development, transportation and consumption were developing at lightning speed. At the same time the market was flooded with new and inventive products made for the growing number of consumers. The advertising industry was born, and new typefaces were needed to make advertisements stand out against those of the competition.

Countless formal experiments took place in the realm of decorative letterforms. The sans-serif typeface – so beloved today and considered current – emerged in the 19th century. The high point of the accentuated serif lay likewise in the Gründerzeit – the foundational era of typography. Alongside the so-called Egyptian typefaces emerged Italian and Etienne.

Typefaces

Decorative typefaces

Characteristics

Kaiserzeit-Gotisch

Named after the fractured appearance of its bowls. Whether used in body text, as decorative script or for highly-wrought initials, it was influential in the 19th century.

Fractured typefaces

Characteristics

Normande

The classical Antique distinguishes itself through the stark contrast between strong ascenders and extremely fine hairline strokes. The axis of its bowls is absolutely perpendicular.

Classical Antique

Characteristics

Egyptientto2

Egyptian evolved from classical Antique and was much used in advertising and marketing. Its serifs are strongly pronounced and appear to the eye almost as strong as its ascenders.

Egyptian

Characteristics

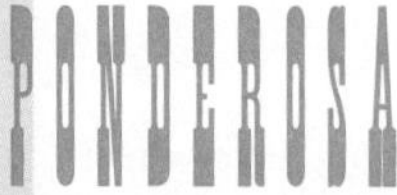

Italian takes the 'accentuated serif' principle to an extreme, so that the serifs end up being very pronounced. It was especially popular in America and is reminiscent of the Wild West.

Italian

Characteristics

Clarendon

In comparison to other scripts with accentuated serifs, Etienne appears rather elegant. Its use of stable serifs resulted in it being much used in 19th-century newsprint.

Etienne

Characteristics

Sans Thirteen

Typefaces without serifs also emerged in the 19th century. They derived from classical Antique and were set mainly in large, uppercase letters.

Sans-serif script

Characteristics

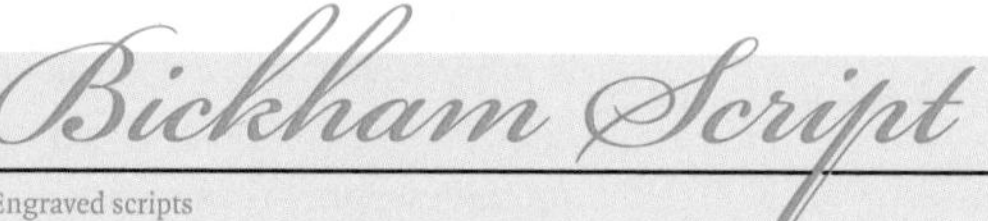

Its form comes from engraving techniques. Mainly the cursive scripts (but also uppercase alphabets) derived from Antique have made it into the digital age.

Engraved scripts

Characteristics

During the 19th century, lithography resulted in the introduction of many decorative typefaces that were used primarily for ornamentation rather than legibility. They were often moulded in plastic.

Characteristics

Example:
Madame
J. Gillé
1820 | page 23

Example:
Bickham Script
Richard Lipton
2000 | page 52

Example:
Sans Thirteen Black
Manfred Klein
2006 | page 63

Example:
Clarendon Black
H. Eidenbenz
1953 | page 69

Example:
Ponderosa
Chansler, Crossgrove
Twombly
1990 | page 66

Example:
Egyptienttо2
Bumbayo Font Fabrik
2005 | page 44

Example:
Normande BT
H. Berthold
1860 | page 19

Example:
Kaiserzeit-Gotisch
Dieter Steffmann
2001 | page 35

Kinds of typefaces

Along with Antique and Fraktur scripts, the following receive wide applications: classical Antique (extra-bold and ultra-condensed); Egyptian, Italian and Etienne; cursive and engraved scripts; calligraphic scripts; Grotesque scripts (in uppercase text); decorative scripts (especially American) and plastic typefaces.

Hybrid scripts/text

Many typefaces result from the combination of existing fonts. Not infrequently, font size changes as well. Often a new font and a different font size are used even in the same line.

Usually fonts are centred. Less frequent are diagonal, circular and bowed arrangements of text. In these cases, decorative styles are preferred.

Ornaments

Historicizing detail, embellished borders and decorative lines are the most popular. Lavish illustration is likewise in fashion.

Aus
RICHARD WAGNER'S LOHENGRIN.
No. I. Festspiel und Brautlied
No. II. Elsa's Traum und Lohengrin's Verweis an Elsa
für das Pianoforte
VON
FRANZ LISZT.

No. I. Festspiel und Brautlied (Neue umgearbeitete Ausgabe.) Pr. Mk. 3.—
„ II. Elsa's Traum und Lohengrin's Verweis an Elsa „ „ 1.50

Neue revidirte Ausgabe.

Eigenthum der Verleger.

Leipzig, Breitkopf & Härtel.

Eingetragen in das Vereinsarchiv.

10343. 8922.

Breitkopf & Härtel
Notebook, c. 1850

JF RINGMASTER

DICKE
BERTA

75 pt

A B C D E F G
H I J K L M
N O P Q R S T
U V W X Y Z
1 2 3 4 5 6 7 8 9 0
„ & ! ? $: ; "

45 pt

JF Ringmaster
Jester Font Studio, 2001
www.dafont.com

CD

THORNE SHADED

ENGRAVED
PROBABLY
ABOUT 1810

15 / 30 pt

ABCD
EFGHIJK
LMNOP
QRSTUVW
XYZ
123&456
7890

30 pt

Thorne Shaded
Dieter Steffmann, 2002
Robert Thorne, c. 1830
www.steffmann.de

CD

NORMANDE BT

Jedermann kann fahren ohne gelernt zu haben in dem auf dem Schaubudenplatze neu konstruierten Amerikanischen Velocipéde-Circus

15 pt

ABCDEFGHI JKLMNOPQRST UVWXYZ abcdefghijklm nopqrstuvwxyzäöü 1234567890 ([„&fiflß!?$£§†"])

36 pt

Normande BT
H. Berthold, 1860
www.bertholdtypes.com

BROADCAST TITLING

TOUR

115 pt

ABCDEFG
HIJKLM
NOPQRST
UVWXYZ
1234567890
ÄÖÜ&!?:;

55 pt

Broadcast Titling
Dieter Steffmann, 2000
Fonderie Deberny Peignot, c. 1830
www.steffmann.de

☞ CD

Lungfish Spring Tour
Poster
Jason Munn, 2003

VERZIERTE MUSIRTE GOTISCH

95 pt

A B C D E F G H I
J K L M N O P Q R S T
U V W X Y Z
a b c d e f g h i j k l m
n o p q r ſ s t u v w x y z
ä ö ü 1 2 3 4 5 6 7 8 9 0
(& ch ck ſch ſt ſi fl tz ß ! ? : ;)

39 pt

Verzierte Musirte Gotisch
Gerhard Helzel, 2002
Gießerei Flinsch, c. 1870
www.romana-hamburg.de

MADAME

DIRNE

100 pt

ABCDEFG
HIJKLM
NOPQRST
UVWXYZ
1234567890
(&!?$£€@:;)

50 pt

Madame
J. Gillé, 1820
www.linotype.com

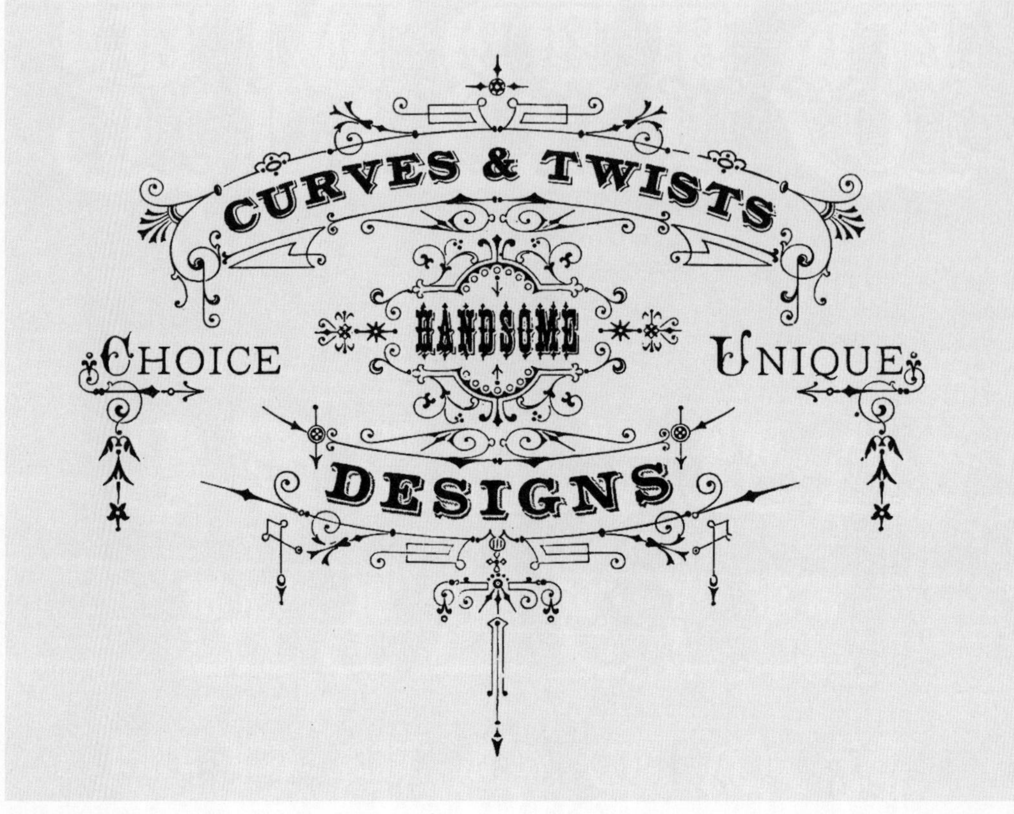

Business card
D. & G. Bruce, 1813

SHADOWED SERIF

BREAK

75 pt

ABCDEFG
HIJKLM
NOPQRST
UVWXYZ
123456
7890

45 pt

Shadowed Serif
James Fordyce, 1994
www.dafont.com

CD

PEPPERWOOD

SATTEL

200 pt

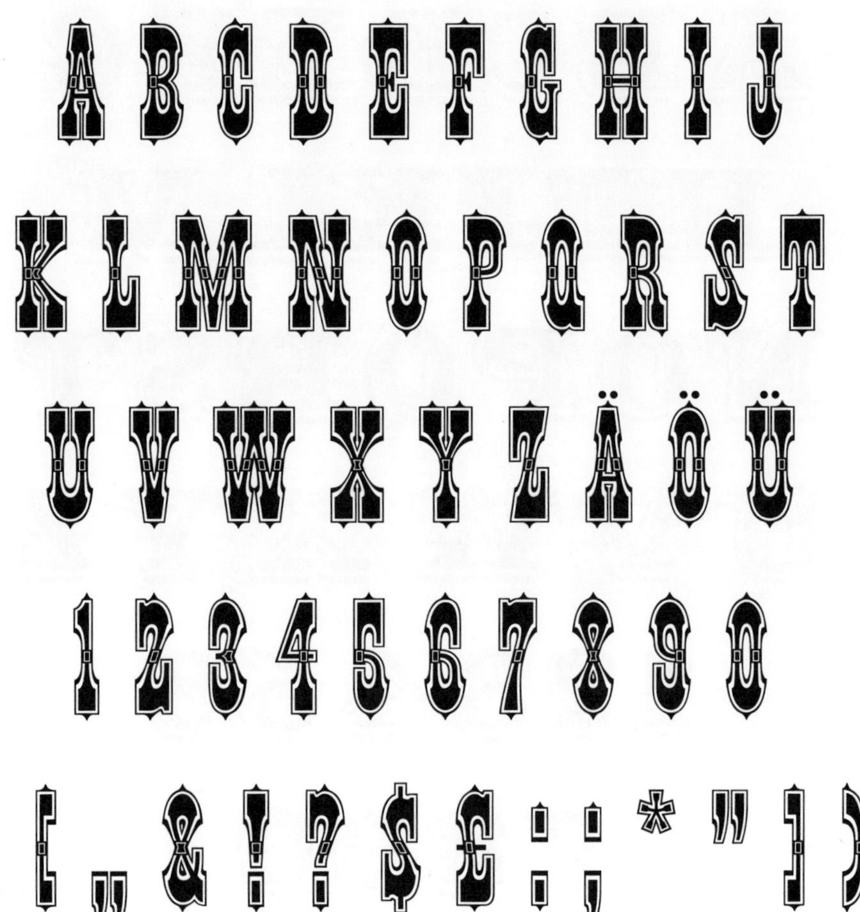

65 pt

Pepperwood
Kim Buker Chansler, Carl Crossgrove,
Carol Twombly, 1994
www.adobe.com/type

ZEBRAWOOD

CLOWN

110 pt

ABCDEFG
HIJKLM
NOPQRST
UVWXYZ
1234567890
(ÄÖÜ&!?$£)

55 pt

Zebrawood
Kim Buker Chansler, Carl Crossgrove,
Carol Twombly, 1994
www.adobe.com/type

MESQUITE

CIRCUS

170 pt

ABCDEFGHIJKLM

NOPQRSTUVWXYZ

ÄÖÜ1234567890

(&!?$£€§†:;)

60 pt

Mesquite
Joy Redick, 1990
www.adobe.com/type

Barbez and the Beat Circus
Poster
Lure Design, c. 2000

ROSEWOOD

POKER

120 pt

ABCDEFG
HIJKLM
NOPQRST
UVWXYZ
1234567890
(ÄÖÜ&!?$£)

55 pt

Rosewood
Kim Buker Chansler, Carl Crossgrove,
Carol Twombly, 1994
www.adobe.com/type

COTTONWOOD

125 pt

ABCDEFG

HIJKLM

NOPQRST

UVWXYZ

1234567890

(ÄÖÜ&!?$£)

45 pt

Cottonwood
Kim Buker Chansler, Carl Crossgrove,
Carol Twombly, 1994
www.adobe.com/type

JOHN T. WHITE,
TYPE AND STEREOTYPE FOUNDER,
No. 45 Gold-street,
(SECOND DOOR SOUTH OF FULTON-STREET,)
New-York,
Invites the attention of Editors and Printers generally to his extensive and unrivalled assortment of
TYPE, FLOWERS
AND
ORNAMENTS,
ALSO
BRASS RULES, CHASES, GALLEYS, CASES,
COMPOSING STICKS, INK,
And every article required in a Printing Office.
He is also Agent for the Napier, Smith, Washington, and Adams' and Ramage's Power and Hand PRESSES.
ALL OF WHICH CAN BE FURNISHED AT SHORT NOTICE.

The reputation of this Foundry is believed to be fully established, having been founded upward of thirty years, and reference is confidently made to many of the leading journals of the United States and the Canadas as to the beauty and durability of the Type.

Orders put up for the South American and Mexican markets, with Spanish, French and Portuguese Accents.

Editors and Printers wishing to establish a Newspaper or Job Printing Office, will be furnished with an estimate in detail for the same, by stating the size of the paper, or the particular style and quantity of work to be executed.

1843.

Type specimen book
John T. White, 1843

JF FERRULE

SALOON

65 pt

ABCDEFGHI
JKLMNOPQR
STUVWXYZ

ABCDEFGHI
JKLMNOPQR
STUVW
XYZ

32 pt

JF Ferrule
Jester Font Studio, 2000
www.dafont.com

☞ CD

GRUSSKARTEN-GOTISCH

Wir leben, das iſt weltbekannt,
Im neunzehnten Jahrhundert.
Wo jeder Tag was neues bringt,
Das Jedermann bewundert.

30 pt

A B C D E F G H I
J K L M N O P Q R S T
U V W X Y Z
a b c d e f g h i j k l m
n o p q r s ſ t u v w x y z ä ö ü
1 2 3 4 5 6 7 8 9 0
(„ & ch ck ! ? $ € † : ; * ")

40 pt

Grusskarten-Gotisch
Dieter Steffmann, 2001
www.steffmann.de

CD

KAISERZEIT-GOTISCH

Kaiſer Wilhelm

63 / 100 pt

A B C D E F G H I
J K L M N O P Q R S T
U V W X Y Z
a b c d e f g h i j k l m
n o p q r s ſ t u v w x y z
ä ö ü ȷ 1 2 3 4 5 6 7 8 9 0
(„ & fi ß ! ? § € † : ; * ")

42 pt

Kaiserzeit-Gotisch
Dieter Steffmann, 2001
Otto Weisert, c. 1900
www.steffmann.de

☞ CD

FT ROSECUBE

KOCHBUCH

90 pt

A B C D E F G

H I J K L M

N O P Q R S T

U V W X Y Z

1 2 3 4 5 6 7 8 9 0

(Ä Ö & ! ? : ;)

60 pt

FT Rosecube
Fenotype Typefaces, 2005
www.fenotype.com

☞ CD

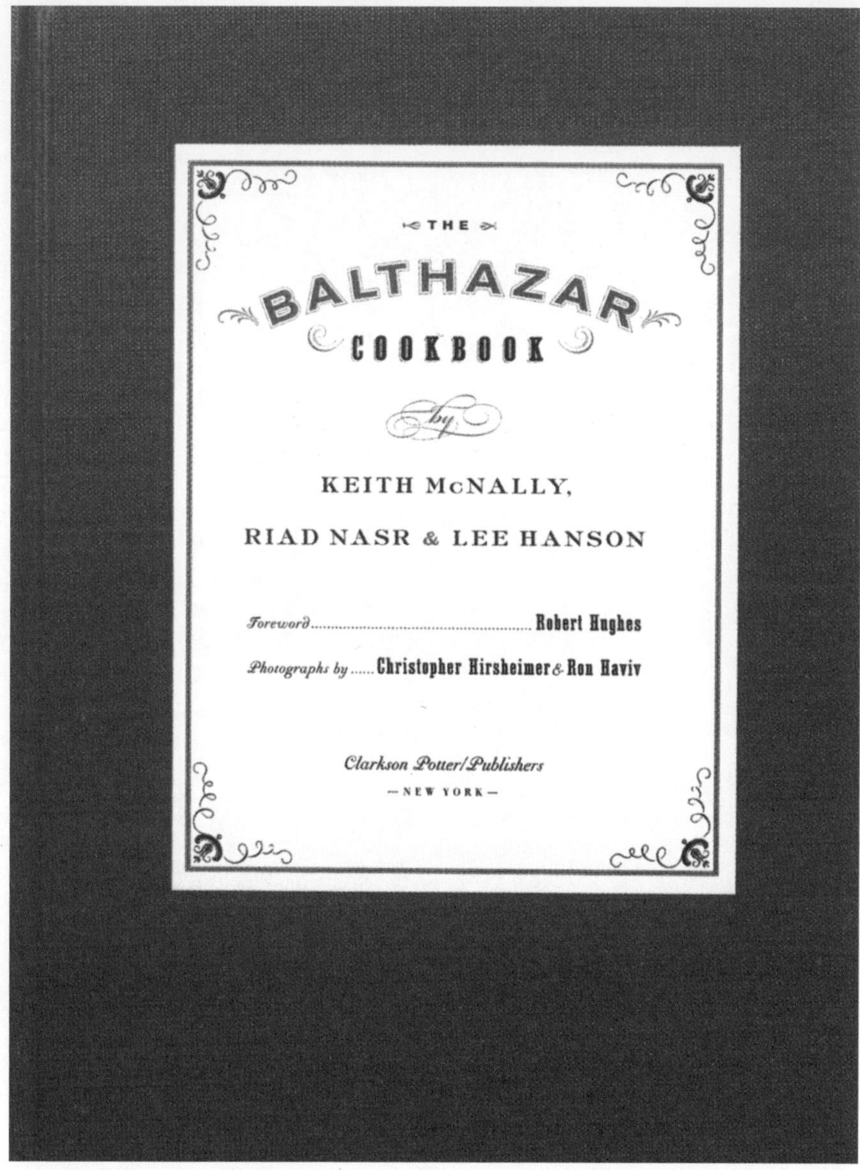

The Balthazar Cookbook
Mucca Design, c. 2000

ENGRAVERS ROMAN

GRAVUR

95 pt

ABCDEFGHI
JKLMNOPQR
STUVWXYZ

ABCDEFGHIJKLM
NOPQRSTUVWXYZ
1234567890ÄÖÜ
([“&!?$£§†:;*”])

40 pt

Engravers Roman
Bitstream, 1990
www.bitstream.com

ENGLISH SCRIPT (100) BOLD

Einladung

90 pt

A B C D E F G H I

J K L M N O P Q R

S T U V W X Y Z

a b c d e f g h i j k l m

n o p q r s t u v w x y z ä ö ü

1 2 3 4 5 6 7 8 9 0

([" & ß ! ? $ £ : ; * "])

35 pt

English Script (100) Bold
Linotype, 2006
www.linotype.com

EIN SECHSTEL THALER 5 GR.

NEUE ZOOLOGISCHE GESELLSCHAFT

Frankfurt a/M.

constituirt
in der General-Versammlung am 31. October 1872.

ACTIE

No 1827

über

Zwei Hundert und Fünfzig Gulden
Süddeutsche Währung

eingetragen in dem Actien-Buche der Gesellschaft auf

Herrn Joh. Conr. Roth

FRANKFURT a. M.

Durch statutengemässe Zuzahlung von Mk. 21.43 S. erhöht auf: Vierhundert und fünfzig Mark
Der Verwaltungsrath.

Der Verwaltungsrath
der Neuen Zoologischen Gesellschaft:

Hierzu 10 Dividenden-Coupons und Talon.

C. Knautz'sche Druckerei, Frankfurt a. M.

Zoological Society
Share certificate
C. Knautz'sche Druckerei, 1872

CIRCUS ORNATE

75 pt

ABCD

EFGHIJK

LMNOP

QRSTUV

WXYZ

32 pt

Circus Ornate
Dieter Steffmann, 2001
www.steffmann.de

☞ CD

COPPERPLATE

ENTREE FÜR ERWACHSENE
6 KREUZER
KINDER UND MILITÄR DIE HÄLFTE,
WO JEDER BESUCHER EINE
FAHRT FREI HAT.

20 / 50 pt

ABCDEFGHI
JKLMNOPQR
STUVWXYZÄÖÜ
ABCDEFGHIJKLM
NOPQRSTUVWXYZ
1234567890
([„&!?$£€§†*"])

45 pt

Copperplate
F. W. Goudy, C. C. Marder, 1901
www.linotype.com

HOMINIS

EISENBAHN

50 pt

ABCDEFG

HIJKLM

NOPQRST

UVWXYZ

1234567890

(" & ! ? : ; ')

40 pt

Hominis
Paul Lloyd, 1997
www.moorstation.org/typoasis/designers/lloyd

EGYPTIENTTO2

ROT

65 pt

ABCDEFGHI

JKLMNOPQR

STUVWXYZ

abcdefghijklm

nopqrstuvwxyz

1234567890

"&!?$:;-

20 pt

Egyptientto2
Bumbayo Font Fabrik, 2005
bumbayo.extra.hu

☞ CD

Binifadet
Wine label
Estudio Duró, 2003

DAMPFPLATZ SHADOW

Black Letter
Engraved

30 / 85 pt

A B C D E F G H I
J K L M N O P Q R S T
V U W X Y Z
a b c d e f g h i j k l m
n o p q r s ſ t u v w x y z
1 2 3 4 5 6 7 8 9 0
" ' & ch ck ſch ß ? ! : ; ' "

40 pt

Dampfplatz Shadow
Paul Lloyd, 2002
www.moorstation.org/typoasis/designers/lloyd

☞ CD

ENGRAVIER INITIALS

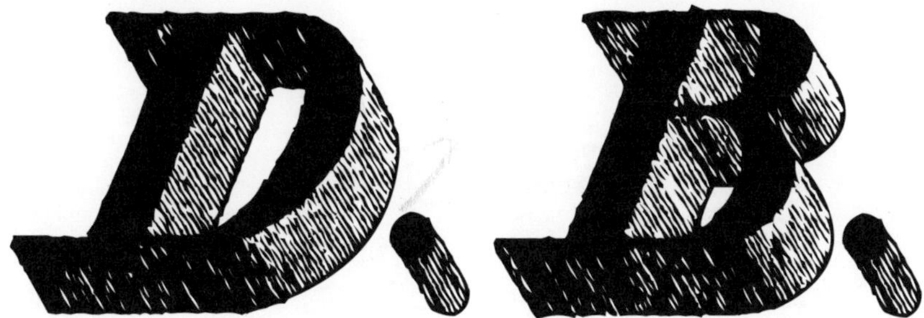

100 pt

ABCDEF
GHIJKLM
NOPQRS
TUVW
XYZ

36 pt

Engravier Initials
Paul Lloyd, 1999
www.moorstation.org/typoasis/designers/lloyd

☞ CD

Business card
D. & G. Bruce, 1818

PLAYBILL

Sheriff

180 pt

A B C D E F G H I J K L M
N O P Q R S T U V W X Y Z
abcdefghijklm
nopqrstuvwxyzäöü
1234567890
([„ & ß ! ? $ £ § "])

55 pt

Playbill
Robert Harling, 1934
www.linotype.com

PLASTISCHE PLAKAT-ANTIQUA

NON PLUS
ULTRA

40 / 120 pt

A B C D E F G
H I J K L M
N O P Q R S T
U V W X Y Z
1 2 3 4 5 6
7 8 9 0

55 pt

Plastische Plakat-Antiqua
Dieter Steffmann, 2002
Gille Fils, 1828
www.steffmann.de

CD

ENGE HOLZSCHRIFT SHADOW

NOCH NIE DAGEWESEN!

60 pt

ABCDEFGHIJKLM
NOPQRSTUVWXYZ
ABCDEFGHIJKLM
NOPQRSTUVWXYZ
1234567890
(„ & ! ? $ £ § † : ; * ”)

50 pt

Enge Holzschrift Shadow
Dieter Steffmann, 2000
www.steffmann.de

CD

BICKHAM SCRIPT

83 pt

ABCDEFGHI

JKLMNOPQRST

UVWXYZ

abcdefghijklm

nopqrstuvwxyzäöü

1234567890 ([&ß!?§†])

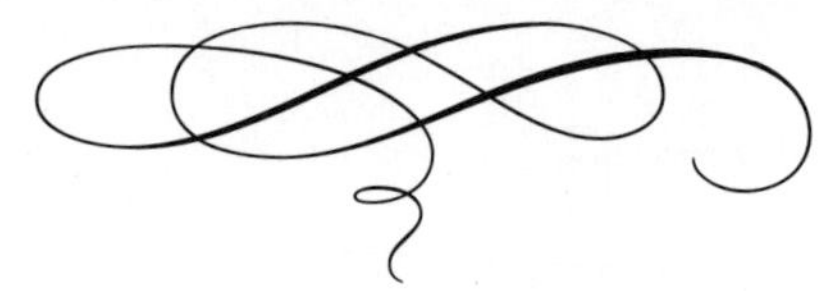

50 pt

Bickham Script
Richard Lipton, 2000
www.adobe.com/type

Perfume
Book cover
John Gall, Gabriele Wilson, c. 2000

LARGE

AUCTION

SALE.

Thursday, July 14.

WILL be sold at the Auction Store, by order of the mortgagee of a bankrupt, a large lot of

TABLE CUTLERY,

GLASS LAMPS,

CROCKERY, CHINA,

BRITANNIA WARE, &C.

150 sets fine table and tea Knives and Folks, 14 sets of Carvers, butchers and bread Knives, 100 pair glass Lamps 120 Waiters, 50 pair Britannia Lamps, Britannia Tea and Coffee Pots, 3 doz. printed and painted Chambers, 20 doz. vegetable Dishes, 22 doz. Bakers, 30 doz. printed Plates, 68 Bowls and Pitchers, 20 doz. Coffee and Tea Sets, 100 printed Pitchers, 6 China Tea Sets.

Also, 15 patent Matrasses.

Sales commence at 9 o'clock, A. M. *Every article must be sold.*

B. & W. HUDSON, Auct'rs.

If the weather is stormy sale first fair day after.

THE

MARTHA WASHINGTON

TEMPERANCE

FAIR,

AT UNION HALL:

Will be continued THIS afternoon and evening, and to-morrow, and will be terminated to-morrow evening.

This Evening the

GLEE CLUB,

Will sing several *Glees, Songs*, &c. Admittance 12½ cents.

October 6th, 1842.

B. & W. Hudson
Poster
Harold Thompson, 1842

PAISLEY CAPS

120 pt

ABCD

EFGHIJK

LMNOP

QRSTUV

WXYZ

1234567890

51 pt

Paisley Caps
House of Lime, 2000
www.dafont.com

☞ CD

LETTRES OMBRÉES ORNÉES

90 pt

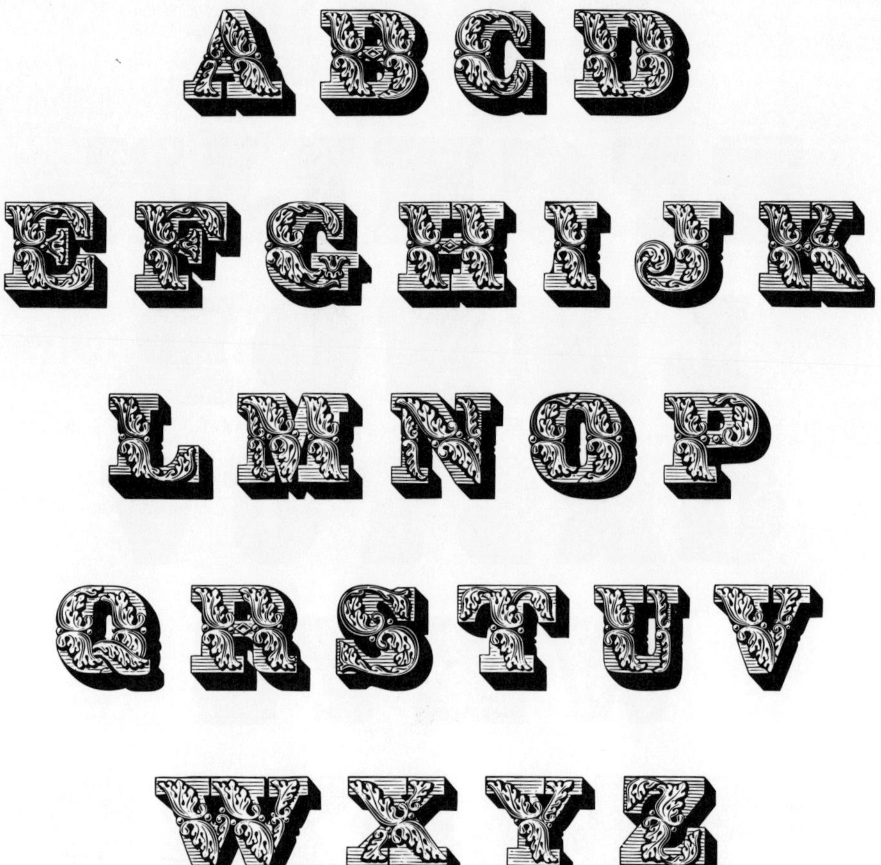

50 pt

Lettres Ombrées Ornées
Dieter Steffmann, 2002
J. Gillié, 1820
www.steffmann.de

☞ CD

Pedro the Lion
Poster
Jason Munn, c. 2000

DEUTSCHE ZIERSCHRIFT

Induſtrie

90 pt

A B C D E F G H I
J K L M N O P Q R S T
U V W X Y Z
a b c d e f g h i j k l m
n o p q r s ſ t u v w x y z ä ö ü
1 2 3 4 5 6 7 8 9 0
(& ſſ ff fi ft ſch ll ch ck ? ! : ;)

35 pt

Deutsche Zierschrift
Dieter Steffmann, 2002
Rudolf Koch, Gebr. Klingspor, 1919
www.steffmann.de

CD

SARABAND INITIALS & LETTERING

80 pt

A B C D E F
G H I J K L M N
O P Q R S T U
V W X Y Z

abcdefghijklm
nopqrstuvwxyz

35 pt

Saraband Initials & Lettering
Paul Lloyd, 2002
www.moorstation.org/typoasis/designers/lloyd

CD

MODERNE KIRCHEN-GOTISCH

50 / 100 pt

A B C D E F G H I

J K L M N O P Q R S T

U V W X Y Z

a b c d e f f g h h i j k l m m

n n o p q r ſ ſ s t u v w x y z

ä ö ü 1 2 3 4 5 6 7 8 9 0

(„ § ch ch ck ff tz ß ! ? : ; “)

35 pt

Moderne Kirchen-Gotisch
Gerhard Helzel, c. 1880
www.romana-hamburg.de

Communicata & *The Book*
Book cover
Lindsey Gice, 2006

EGYPTIAN (100) BOLD CONDENSED

Brandzeichen

80 pt

ABCDEFGHIJKLM

NOPQRSTUVWXYZ

abcdefghijklm

nopqrstuvwxyzäöü

1234567890

(&ß!?$£€@:;*)

45 pt

Egyptian (100) Bold Condensed
Tetterode Foundry, c. 1820
www.linotype.com

SANS THIRTEEN BLACK

Lederware

80 pt

ABCDEFGHIJKLM
NOPQRSTUVWXYZ
abcdefghijklm
nopqrstuvwxyzäöü
1234567890
(&fiß!?$£€§†:;*)

45 pt

Sans Thirteen Black
Manfred Klein, 2006
www.moorstation.org/typoasis/designers/klein

CD

Non plus ultra!

Noch nie dagewesen.

Jedermann kann fahren ohne gelernt zu haben während der Messe in dem auf dem Schaubudenplatze neu construirten

Amerikanischen

Velocipéde-Circus

von

J. JÄGER.

NON PLUS ULTRA!

Noch nie dagewesen!

Während der Messe
geöffnet von
Morgens bis Abends.
Entrée à Person 6 kr.

In der
großen Bretter-Arena
von
Morgens bis Abends.
Entrée à Person 6 kr.

Wir leben, das ist weltbekannt,
Im neunzehnten Jahrhundert,
Wo jeder Tag was neues bringt,
Das Jedermann bewundert.
D'rum zogen wir von Engeland
Hieher zum schönen deutschen Strand,
Dass Jedermann sich amüsirt,
Sich amüsirt für wenig Geld,
Was noch nie dagewesen.

Ihr könnt's auf unserm Bilde seh'n
Und in der Zeitung lesen;
Weil Ihr nun wisst, dass Messe ist,
So seid bei frohem Muthe,
Und lös't Euch schleunigst ein Billet
Zum Jäger'schen Institute,
Wo sich auf Velocipeden
Die Damen produciren,
Und Herren dabei und obendrein

Lässt Jäger auch musiciren.
D'rum kommt herbei und säumet nicht
Und achtet auf die Hunde,
Denn leicht Malheur für diese ist
Das Jagen in die Runde;
Und seid auf Alles gut bedacht,
Und macht mir kein Spectakel,
Denn 6 Kreuzer sind ja nichts
Für diesen Tabernakel!!

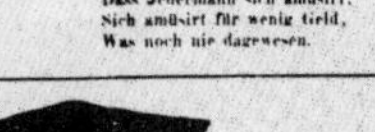

Entree für Erwachsene 6 kr.

Kinder und Militär die Hälfte, wo jeder Besucher eine Fahrt frei hat.

Für Damen und Kinder sind extra gepolsterte Damensitze vorhanden, wo man bequem und ohne Gefahr reiten und fahren kann.

Abends bei brillanter Beleuchtung.

Zu diesem niemals dagewesenen Vergnügen ladet ergebenst ein

J. Jäger.

Oktoberfest
Poster, 1881

THOROWGOOD

Festwiese

70 pt

ABCDEFGHI
JKLMNOPQRST
UVWXYZ
abcdefghijklm
nopqrstuvwxyz
1234567890
(äöü&ß!?$£:;)

40 pt

Thorowgood
William Thorowgood, 1836
www.linotype.com

PONDEROSA

SCHWERVERBRECHER

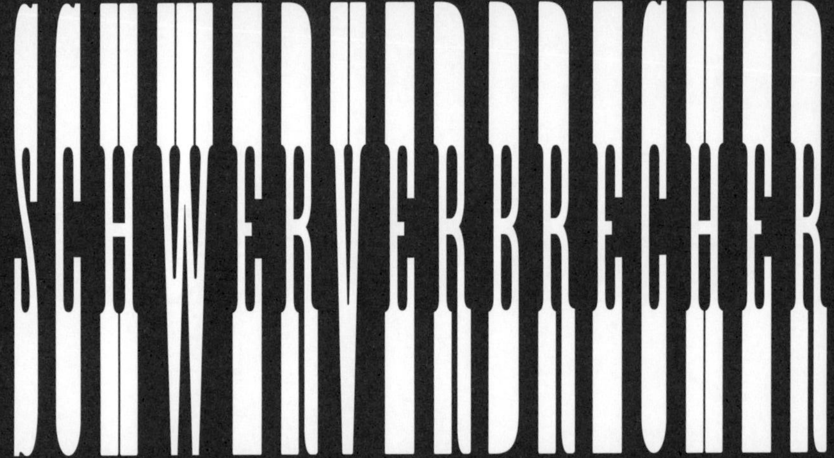

200 pt

A B C D E F G H I J K L M

N O P Q R S T U V W X Y Z Ä Ö Ü

1 2 3 4 5 6 7 8 9 0

([„ & ! ? $ £ : ; * ”])

76 pt

Ponderosa
Kim Buker Chansler, Carl Crossgrove,
Carol Twombly, 1990
www.adobe.com/type

Eleven Productions
Poster
Brady Vest, 2006

FETTE EGYPTIENNE

Wanted

75 pt

ABCDEFGHI
JKLMNOPQR
STUVWXYZ
abcdefghijklm
nopqrstuvwxyz
1234567890äöü
([„&ß!?$£§†:;*"])

32 pt

Fette Egyptienne
Dieter Steffmann, 2001
www.steffmann.de

CD

CLARENDON BLACK

D'rum kommt herbei und säumet nicht
Und achtet auf die Hunde,
Denn leicht Malheur für diese ist
Das Jagen in die Runde.

18 pt

A B C D E F G H I
J K L M N O P Q R S T
U V W X Y Z
a b c d e f g h i j k l m
n o p q r s t u v w x y z
1 2 3 4 5 6 7 8 9 0
(ä ö ü & fi fl ß ! ? $ £)

36 pt

Clarendon Black
H. Eidenbenz, 1953
www.linotype.com

JUG
END
STIL

Eckmann
Otto Eckmann
1900 | page 86

Reynold Art Deco
Dieter Steffmann
2000 | page 125

Art Nouveau

1890 — 1918

Ira Rubel with the offset printing press he developed in 1904

2

Fin de Siècle and Simplicissimus Art Nouveau and Japonism

c. 1890–1918

In the arts, a new movement developed that demanded new principles of design and began to reject the products of historicism. Art Nouveau is the avant-garde movement of the period in reaction to historical and academic perspectives. It is characterized by its elegant style, detailed patterns, curving lines and art innovation

XIX. Jahrgang, Heft 24 15. September 1904

DIE KUNST FÜR ALLE

Herausgegeben von F. Schwartz

INHALT:

Die Münchener Jahresausſtellung im Glaspalaſte. Von Franz Wolter · Die „Fine Arts" auf der Weltausſtellung in St. Louis. Von Dr. Max Creutz · Der preußiſche Staat als Käufer von Kunſtwerken. Von W. Wygodzinski

• • •

Perſonal- und Atelier-Nachrichten · Von Ausſtellungen und Sammlungen · Vermiſchtes

• • •

SONDERBEILAGE:

F. A. v. Kaulbach, Eine Mutter (Gravüre)

VERLAGSANSTALT
F. BRUCKMANN A.-G.
IN MÜNCHEN

Preis vierteljährlich 3 M. 60 Pfg. • Monatlich zwei Hefte. • Einzelpreis des Heftes 1 M.
Zu beziehen durch alle Buchhandlungen und Poſtanſtalten.

Die Kunst für Alle
Magazine cover
F. Bruckmann A.-G., 1904

Fin de Siècle and Simplicissimus
Art Nouveau and Japonism

c. 1890–1918

Arnold Böcklin
Arnold Böcklin
1904 | page 78

KRAFT LINIE

Type design itself emanates primarily from painters and architects and new forms of typefaces emerge, uninfluenced by professional expertise and formal education. In contrast to the historicizing typefaces of the Gründerzeit, the variants of Fraktur – a formally hybrid interplay of Antique and Fraktur – constitute something fundamentally new. They are clearly rooted in Art Nouveau, though their dark and angular typeface reveals a kinship with Fraktur.

Besides innumerable variations on Antique, which often resemble scripts written with a brush, Art Nouveau gave birth also to sans-serif handwritten styles that conform to obviously geometric considerations: willful, blocky lettering whose elements are aligned on a square or rectangular field. These are combined yet again in square or rectangular patterns, so that a grid-like, geometric text is generated.

The decorative scripts of Art Nouveau are fully free, exceptionally flat and experimental. They make reference to illustrations or ornaments, and they are made out of ornaments or as ornaments. In poster art the script becomes fully integrated into the overall poster. Image and text enter into an alliance and achieve compositional unity.

Typefaces

Behrens-Schrift

Variants of Fraktur

These variants of Fraktur, which represent a hybrid form of Fraktur and Antique, clearly have roots in Art Nouveau. Their energetic, powerful form was extremely popular in commercial printing.

Characteristics

ART NOUVEAU

Decorative scripts

The decorative scripts were designed at the turn of the century more as ornaments, or rather from ornaments. Their form usually mirrored the context in which they were set.

Characteristics

Hobo

Poster scripts

Typefaces that were more legible than decorative scripts were used for advertisements, commercial signs and posters. Formally, however, they were testaments to their time.

Characteristics

Auriol

Brushed scripts

Though their basic structures resemble Antique, the brushed scripts take their inspiration also from Japanese calligraphy. Their characteristic style is of script rendered with a paintbrush.

Characteristics

ADRESACK

San-serif handwritten scripts

The letters of the sans-serif handwritten scripts are aligned on square or rectangular fields. The median line is often shifted much higher or lower.

Characteristics

Characteristics

Example:
Behrens-Schrift
Dieter Steffmann
2002 | page 103

Example:
Art Nouveau Caps
Dieter Steffmann
1999 | page 79

Example:
Hobo
Morris Fuller Benton
1910 | page 91

Example:
Auriol
Georges Auriol
1901 | page 104

Example:
Adresack
David Nalle
1993 | page 85

Typefaces

The new inventions of the time – variants on Fraktur and Antique, handwritten scripts and decorative scripts in the spirit of Art Nouveau – were to be used for title pages, book covers and other similar applications. Both Antique and Fraktur scripts were frequently used for body text.

Experimental Typography

Experimental typography rendered with the new typefaces was cramped and set in capital letters. In order to achieve the proper balance, typographers and artists employed extravagant ligatures or designed individual letters. Block lettering was popular in layouts. Text was divided up into groups, each of which was set in a block. The groups were then placed in turn on the central axis. Illustrations or embellished details with centred borders were also popular.

Ornaments

Nature was a frequent source of inspiration for ornamentation: lilies – especially water lilies – and ivy leaves were used in a stylized manner by the typesetter. Lines were frequently employed as decorative elements in shop signs and book design. Floral borders or stylized plants enclosed columns of text and type areas. Illustrated initials were often used and borders were richly ornamented.

Paris Metro, c. 1900
Entrance signs typeface by
Hector Guimard

METROPOLITAINES

METRO

120 pt

ABCDEFGH

IJKLMNOPQR

STUVWXYZ

1234567890

ÄÖÜ&!?$€@:;

55 pt

Metropolitaines
Hector Guimard, c. 1905
www.linotype.com

ARNOLD BÖCKLIN

Volksbad

90 pt

ABCDEFGHI
JKLMNOPQRST
UVWXYZ
abcdefghijklm
nopqrstuvwxyz
äöü1234567890
(„&fiflß!?$£§*:;)

40 pt

Arnold Böcklin
Arnold Böcklin, 1904
www.linotype.com

ART NOUVEAU CAPS

KRAFT
LINIE

30 / 110 pt

ABCD
EFGHIJK
LMNOP
QRSTUVW
XYZ
1234567890
ÄÖÜ(!?)

40 pt

Art Nouveau Caps
Dieter Steffmann, 1999
www.steffmann.de

CD

RENNIE MACKINTOSH

SCHOKOLADE

85 pt

ABCDEFGHIJKLM

NOPQRSTUVWXYZ

ABCDEFGHIJKLM

NOPQRSTUVWXYZ

ÄÖÜ1234567890

(&&ßTT!?$£€:;)

50 pt

Rennie Macintosh
Phill Grimshaw, 1996
after Charles Rennie Macintosh
www.linotype.com

Moser-Roth
Chocolate bar packaging, c. 2000

HOHENZOLLERN

DIE Herausgeber halten es an dieser Stelle nicht für angebracht, ein Langes und Breites über das vorzubringen, was sie im Rahmen des vorliegenden Heftes alles bieten und erreichen wollen.

18 pt

ABCDEFGHI
JKLMNOPQRST
UVWXYZ
abcdefghijklm
nopqrsſtuvwxyzäöü
1234567890
(„&ſtchckßß!?“)

40 pt

Hohenzollern
Petra Heidorn, 2004
Bauersche Gießerei, 1902
www.moorstation.org/typoasis/blackletter

CD

ROLAND

Die Insel

90 pt

ABCDEFGHI
JKLMNOPQRST
UVWXYZ
abcdefghijklm
nopqrstuvwxyzäöü
1234567890
(„&fiß!?$†“)

35 pt

Roland
Dieter Steffmann, 2000
www.steffmann.de

CD

Darmstadt Künstler-Kolonie
Poster
Josef Maria Olbrich, 1901

ADRESACK

KOLONIE

140 pt

ABCDEFGHIJKLM
NOPQRSTUVWXYZ

ABCDEFGHIJKLM
NOPQRSTUVWXYZ
1234567890
("!?:;*')

45 pt

Adresack
David Nalle, 1993
www.fontcraft.com

ECKMANN

Unter dem allerhöchsten Protectorate
der königlichen Hoheit des Großherzogs
von Hessen ein Dokument
Deutscher Kunst

25 pt

A B C D E F G H I
J K L M N O P Q R
S T U V W X Y Z
a b c d e f g h i j k l m
n o p q r s t u v w x y z ä ö ü
1 2 3 4 5 6 7 8 9 0
(„ & ß ! ? $ € @ : ; ")

43 pt

Eckmann
Otto Eckmann, 1900
www.linotype.com

AUGSBURGER SCHRIFT

Augusta Vindelicum

55 pt

ABCDEFGHI
JKLMNOPQRST
UVWXYZ
abcdefghijklm
nopqrsſtuvwxyzäöü
1234567890
Et ß № ! ? $ @

38 pt

Augsburger Schrift
HiH, after a 1902 model
www.hihretro.com

Künstler-Vignetten

Original-Erzeugnis
Gesetzlich geschützt

1308
Ein- und zweifarbig

1317
Ein- und zweifarbig

1309
Ein- und zweifarbig

1311
Ein- und zweifarbig

1310
Ein- und zweifarbig

1277
Ein- und
zweifarbig

1318

1276
Ein- und
zweifarbig

Anschluß an Halbpetit fette Linien sowie an Künstlerlinien Serie 1

INITIALS WITH CURLS

RAT

160 pt

ABCD
EFGHIJK
LMNOP
QRSTUVW
XYZ

60 pt

Initials with Curls
dnor, 2007
www.dafont.com

CD

HEROLD REKLAMESCHRIFT

Reklame

170 pt

ABCDEFGHIJKLM

NOPQRSTUVWXYZ

abcdefghijklm

nopqrstuvwxyz

äöü1234567890

(“&ß!?$£§:;”)

50 pt

Herold Reklameschrift
Dieter Steffmann, 2002
Heinz Hoffmann, 1904
www.steffmann.de

CD

HOBO

Der liebe Augustin

50 / 85 pt

ABCDEFGHI
JKLMNOPQRST
UVWXYZ
abcdefghijklm
nopqrstuvwxyzäöü
1234567890
(„ & fi fl ! ? $ £ * ")

35 pt

Hobo
Morris Fuller Benton, 1910
www.linotype.com

Ver Sacrum
Poster
Koloman Moser, 1902

KRAMER

VER SACRUM

85 pt

43 pt

Kramer
Dieter Steffmann, 2003
www.steffmann.de

☞ CD

EPOQUE

Rendezvous

110 pt

ABCDEFGHI
JKLMNOPQR
STUVWXYZ
abcdefghijklm
nopqrstuvwxyzäöü
1234567890
(„&ß!?*$£@:;“)

40 pt

Epoque
Dieter Steffmann, 1999
www.steffmann.de

☞ CD

CARRICK CAPS

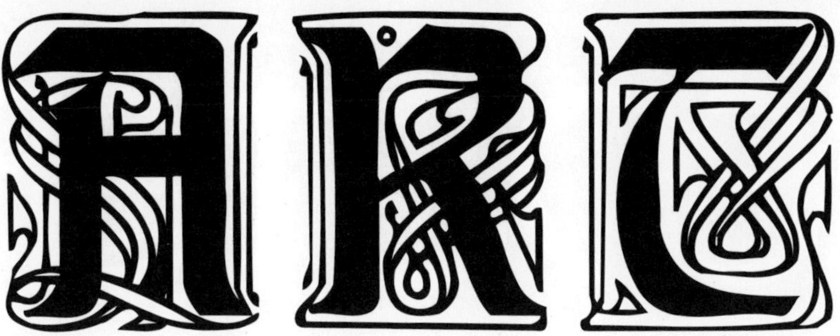

110 pt

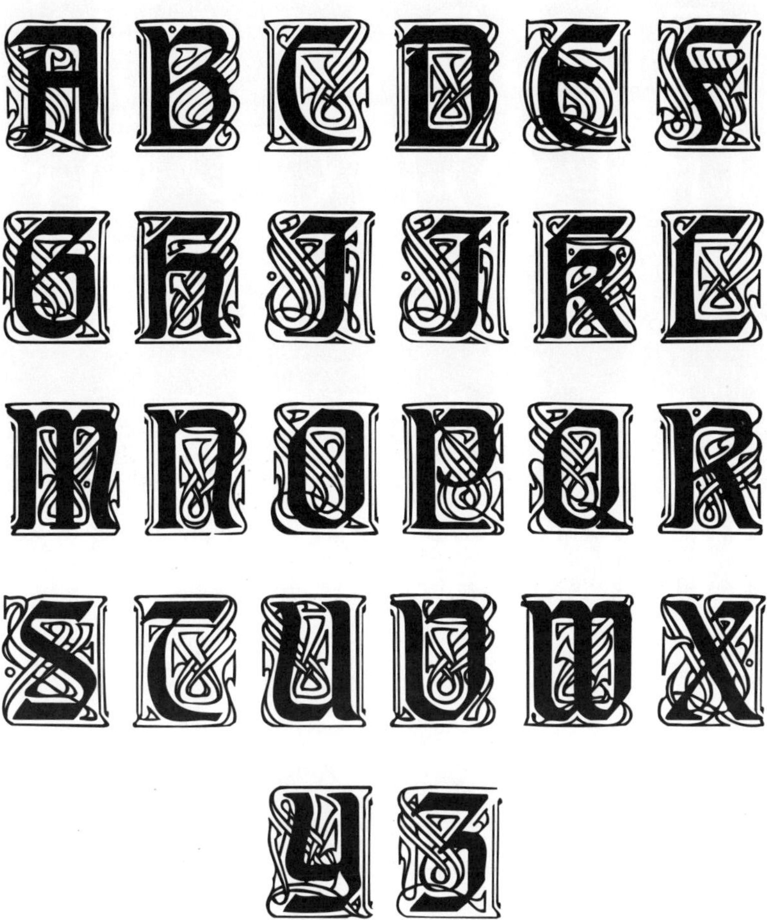

50 pt

Carrick Caps
Dieter Steffmann, 2000
www.steffmann.de

CD

HADLEY

FENSTER

95 pt

ABCDEFGHI
JKLMNOPQR
STUVWXYZÄÖÜ
ABCDEFGHI
JKLMNOPQR
STUVWXYZ
([”&ß$@™§†:;*”])

40 pt

Hadley
Fleisch & Apostrophic Labs, 2005
Ned Hadley, 1916
moorstation.org/typoasis/designers/lab

CD

Shop window
Berlin, 2008

BALDUR

Soeben gelangte zur Aufgabe und iſt
durch alle Buchhandlungen des In- und Auslandes
zu beziehen: das überaus reich illuſtrierte 1. Heft
von Deutſche Kunſt und Dekoration

20 pt

ABCDEFGHI
JKLMNOPQRST
UVWXYZ
abcdefghijklm
nopqrsſtuvwxyzäöü
1234567890
(& fi ſch ß ! ? $ £ ™)

40 pt

Baldur
Dieter Steffmann, 2000
Schriftgießerei Julius Klinkhardt, 1900
www.steffmann.de

CD

CARMEN

Eine neue, eigenartige, äußerſt vornehm ausgeſtaltete Zeitſchrift für Künſtler und

Kunſtfreunde

20 / 65 pt

ABCDEFGHI

JKLMNOPQRST

UVWXYZ

abcdefghijklm

nopqrsſtuvwxyzäöü

1234567890

(„&fißchck!?$£@")

43 pt

WILLOW

PSYCHOLOGIE

100 pt

ABCDEFGHIJK

LMNOPQRSTU

VWXYZÄÖÜ

1234567890

(&!?$£€:;)

60 pt

Willow
Tom Forster, 1993
www.linotype.com

The Future of an Illusion
Book cover, David Pearson, 2004

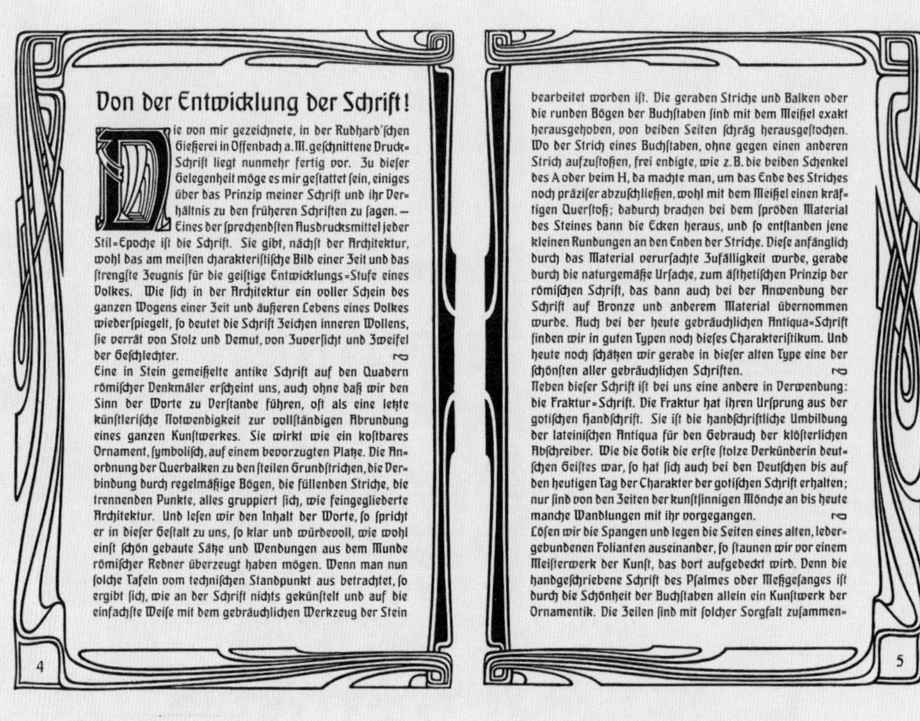

Von der Entwicklung der Schrift!

Die von mir gezeichnete, in der Rudhard'schen Gießerei in Offenbach a. M. geschnittene Druck-Schrift liegt nunmehr fertig vor. Zu dieser Gelegenheit möge es mir gestattet sein, einiges über das Prinzip meiner Schrift und ihr Verhältnis zu den früheren Schriften zu sagen. – Eines der sprechendsten Ausdrucksmittel jeder Stil-Epoche ist die Schrift. Sie gibt, nächst der Architektur, wohl das am meisten charakteristische Bild einer Zeit und das strengste Zeugnis für die geistige Entwicklungs-Stufe eines Volkes. Wie sich in der Architektur ein voller Schein des ganzen Wogens einer Zeit und äußeren Lebens eines Volkes wiederspiegelt, so deutet die Schrift Zeichen inneren Wollens, sie verrät von Stolz und Demut, von Zuversicht und Zweifel der Geschlechter.

Eine in Stein gemeißelte antike Schrift auf den Quadern römischer Denkmäler erscheint uns, auch ohne daß wir den Sinn der Worte zu Verstande führen, oft als eine letzte künstlerische Notwendigkeit zur vollständigen Abrundung eines ganzen Kunstwerkes. Sie wirkt wie ein kostbares Ornament, symbolisch, auf einem bevorzugten Platze. Die Anordnung der Querbalken zu den steilen Grundstrichen, die Verbindung durch regelmäßige Bögen, die füllenden Striche, die trennenden Punkte, alles gruppiert sich, wie feingegliederte Architektur. Und lesen wir den Inhalt der Worte, so spricht er in dieser Gestalt zu uns, so klar und würdevoll, wie wohl einst schön gebaute Sätze und Wendungen aus dem Munde römischer Redner überzeugt haben mögen. Wenn man nun solche Tafeln vom technischen Standpunkt aus betrachtet, so ergibt sich, wie an der Schrift nichts gekünstelt und auf die einfachste Weise mit dem gebräuchlichen Werkzeug der Stein

4

bearbeitet worden ist. Die geraden Striche und Balken oder die runden Bögen der Buchstaben sind mit dem Meißel exakt herausgehoben, von beiden Seiten schräg herausgestochen. Wo der Strich eines Buchstaben, ohne gegen einen anderen Strich aufzustoßen, frei endigte, wie z. B. die beiden Schenkel des A oder beim H, da machte man, um das Ende des Striches noch präziser abzuschließen, wohl mit dem Meißel einen kräftigen Querstoß; dadurch brachen bei dem spröden Material des Steines dann die Ecken heraus, und so entstanden jene kleinen Rundungen an den Enden der Striche. Diese anfänglich durch das Material verursachte Zufälligkeit wurde, gerade durch die naturgemäße Ursache, zum ästhetischen Prinzip der römischen Schrift, das dann auch bei der Anwendung der Schrift auf Bronze und anderem Material übernommen wurde. Auch bei der heute gebräuchlichen Antiqua-Schrift finden wir in guten Typen noch dieses Charakteristikum. Und heute noch schätzen wir gerade in dieser alten Type eine der schönsten aller gebräuchlichen Schriften.

Neben dieser Schrift ist bei uns eine andere in Verwendung: die Fraktur-Schrift. Die Fraktur hat ihren Ursprung aus der gotischen Handschrift. Sie ist die handschriftliche Umbildung der lateinischen Antiqua für den Gebrauch der klösterlichen Abschreiber. Wie die Gotik die erste stolze Verkünderin deutschen Geistes war, so hat sich auch bei den Deutschen bis auf den heutigen Tag der Charakter der gotischen Schrift erhalten; nur sind von den Zeiten der kunstsinnigen Mönche an bis heute manche Wandlungen mit ihr vorgegangen.

Lösen wir die Spangen und legen die Seiten eines alten, ledergebundenen Folianten auseinander, so staunen wir vor einem Meisterwerk der Kunst, das dort aufgedeckt wird. Denn die handgeschriebene Schrift des Psalmes oder Meßgesanges ist durch die Schönheit der Buchstaben allein ein Kunstwerk der Ornamentik. Die Zeilen sind mit solcher Sorgfalt zusammen-

5

Behrens-Schrift
Sample double-page spread, c. 1900

BEHRENS-SCHRIFT

Die Münchner Jahresausſtellung im

Glaspalaſte

25 / 85 pt

ABCDEFGHI
JKLMNOPQRST
UVWXYZ
abcdefghijklm
nopqrsſtuvwxyzäöü
1234567890
& fi fl ß tz ſſ ſt ſch ! ? € @

43 pt

Behrens-Schrift
Dieter Steffmann, 2002
Peter Behrens, 1901
www.steffmann.de

☞ CD

AURIOL

Japonismus

75 pt

ABCDEFGHI
JKLMNOPQRST
UVWXYZ
abcdefghijklm
nopqrstuvwxyzäöü
1234567890
(&ﬁﬂß!?$£†:;)

40 pt

Auriol
Georges Auriol, 1901
www.linotype.com

MENUETTO

Kalligraphie

80 pt

ABCDEFGHI
JKLMNOPQRST
UVWXYZ
abcdefghijklm
nopqrstuvwxyzäöü
1234567890
(„&fiflß!?§¶:;“)

47 pt

Menuetto
Keith Field, 1994
www.dafont.com

☞ CD

Marianne Steinberger. 1109 Kalenderblätter.

Ver Sacrum
Calendar, 1900

HERKULES

Dezember

105 pt

ABCDEFGHI
JKLMNOPQR
STUVWXYZ
abcdefghijklm
nopqrstuvwxyzäöü
1234567890
(„ & ſch ch ck ß ! ? @ : ; * “)

43 pt

Herkules
Dieter Steffmann, 2004
www.steffmann.de

CD

RIVANNA

NEW ART

140 pt

ABCDEFGHI

JKLMNOPQR

STUVWXYZÄÖÜ

äöü1234567890

(„&§!?$£@:;“)

49 pt

Rivanna
Nick Curtis, 2002
www.nicksfonts.com

[illegible] CD

Days of Reading Marcel Proust
Book cover
David Pearson, 2004

MULIER MODERNE

MODERN

85 pt

ABCDEFG

HIJKLMNO

PQRSTUV

WXYZÄÖÜ

1234567890

&!?$£€@

48 pt

Mulier Moderne
E. Mulier, 1894
www.hihretro.com

VOLAN

DEKORA

85 pt

ABCD
EFGHIJK
LMNOP
QRSTUV
WXYZ

55 pt

Volan
Bartek Nowak, 2002
www.nowak.tv/fontoholic

CD

ISADORACAPS

105 pt

ABCDEF
GHIJKLMN
OPQRSTU
VWXYZ
1234567890
(&!? :;)

60 pt

IsadoraCaps
1997
www.dafont.com

CD

Giacondi
Wine label, c. 2000

KONANUR KAPS

LUX

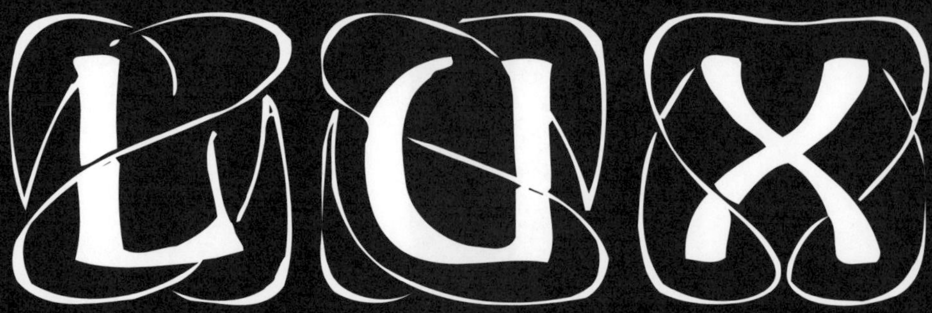

110 pt

ABCDEF
GHIJKL
MNOPQR
STUVW
XYZ

50 pt

Konanur Kaps
Dieter Steffmann, 2000
David Rakowski, 1991
www.steffmann.de

CD

SAN REMO

R8UM

180 pt

ABCDEFGHI
JKLMNOPQRST
UVWXYZÄÖÜ
1234567890
(&!?)

50 pt

San Remo
Dieter Steffmann, 2002
www.steffmann.de

CD

Das Interieur
Book cover, 1908

AMBROSIA

DER
ARCHITEKT

50 / 90 pt

A B C D E F G H I
J K L M N O P Q R
S T U V W X Y Z
abcdefghijklm
nopqrstuvwxyzäöü
1 2 3 4 5 6 7 8 9 0
(„ & fiß ! ? $ £ † : ; * ")

40 pt

Ambrosia
Dieter Steffmann, 2000
www.steffmann.de

CD

CABARET

THEATER

120 pt

ABCDEFGHI
JKLMNOPQR
STUVWXYZ
ÄÖÜ1234567890
(„&!?$£†:;")

51 pt

Cabaret
Dieter Steffmann, 2000
www.steffmann.de

☞ CD

Purple Haze
Logo
C100 Purple Haze, 2006

JUGENDSTIL ORNAMENTE

180 pt

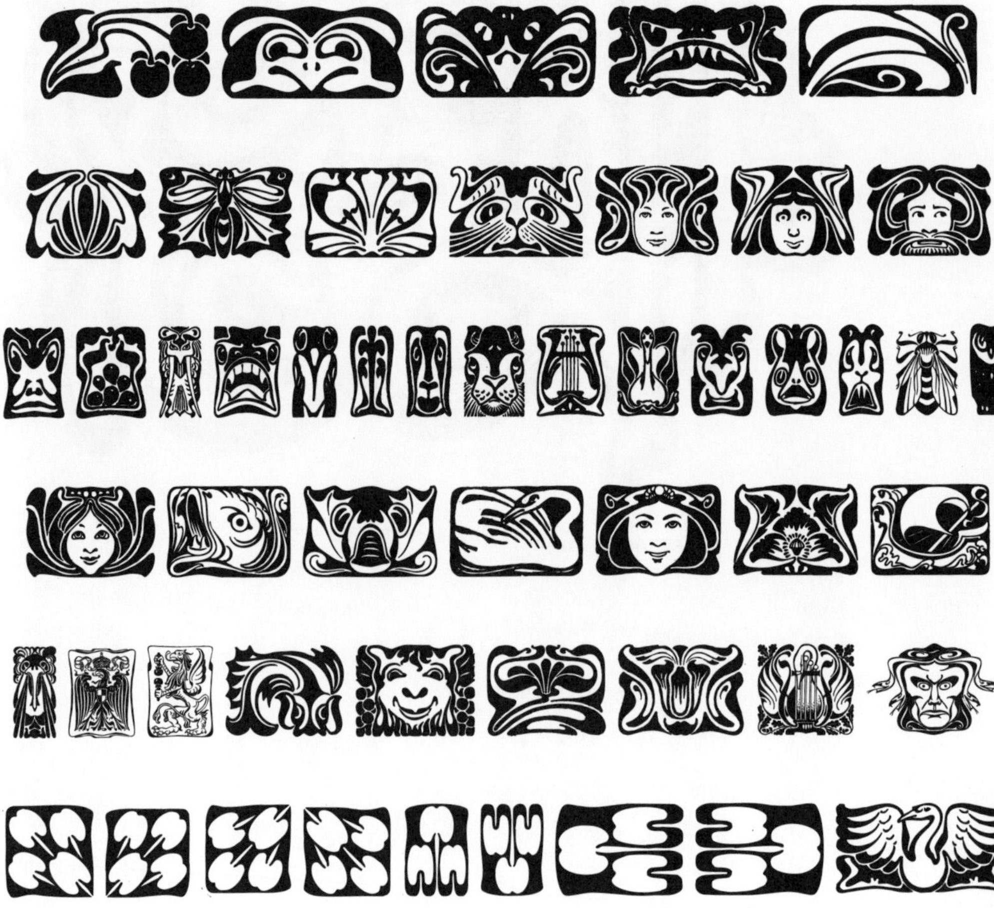

43 pt

Jugendstil Ornamente
Dieter Steffmann, 2002
Schriftgießerei J. G. Schelter & Giesecke, c. 1900
www.steffmann.de

☞ CD

KINIGSTEIN CAPS

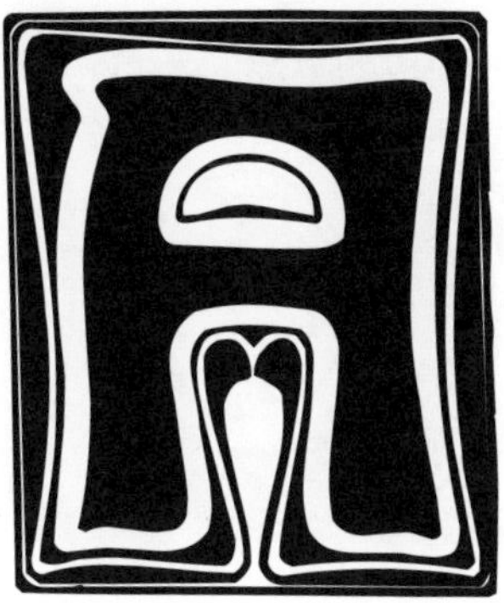

130 pt

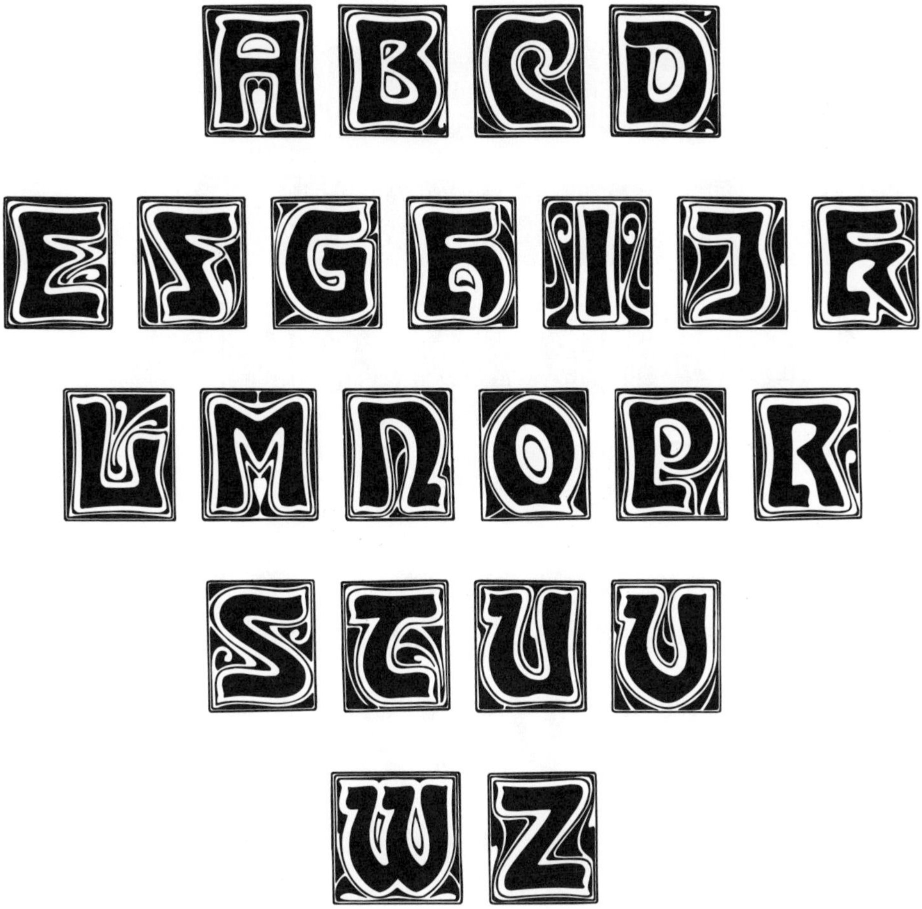

ABCD

EFGHIJK

LMNOPR

STUV

WZ

50 pt

Kinigstein Caps
Dieter Steffmann, 2000
David Rakowski, 1990
www.steffmann.de

CD

RUDELSBERG-INITIALEN

120 pt

ABCDEFGHI
JKLMNOPQRS
TUVWXYZ

ABCDEFGHI
JKLMNOPQRS
TUVWXYZ
(„Ü&!?€“)

35 pt

Rudelsberg-Initialen
Dieter Steffmann, 2002
Otto Eckmann, c. 1900
www.steffmann.de

☞ CD

RUDELSBERG-SCHMUCK

150 pt

48 pt

Rudelsberg-Schmuck
Dieter Steffmann. 2002
Otto Eckmann, c. 1900
www.steffmann.de

CD

TITRES DE COUVERTURES 301

F. THIBAUDEAU, AUTEUR DE "LA LETTRE D'IMPRIMERIE"

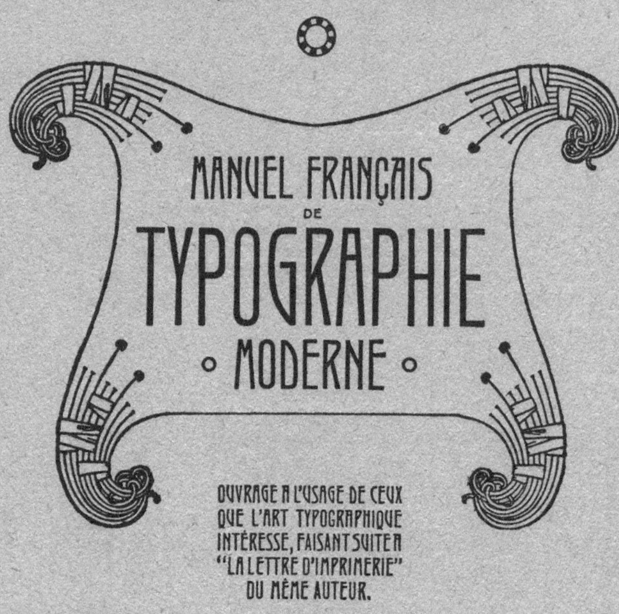

MANUEL FRANÇAIS
DE
TYPOGRAPHIE
MODERNE

OUVRAGE A L'USAGE DE CEUX
QUE L'ART TYPOGRAPHIQUE
INTÉRESSE, FAISANT SUITE A
"LA LETTRE D'IMPRIMERIE"
DU MÊME AUTEUR.

A PARIS
AU BUREAU DE L'ÉDITION
4, AVENUE REILLE

Manuel Français de Typographie Moderne
Title page
F. Thibaudeau, 1924

REYNOLD ART DECO

DEKORATION

100 pt

ABCDEFGHI
JKLMNOPQR
STUVWXYZ
ÄÖÜ1234567890
(„&!?$£©@§†:;*")

50 pt

Reynold Art Deco
Dieter Steffmann, 2000
www.steffmann.de

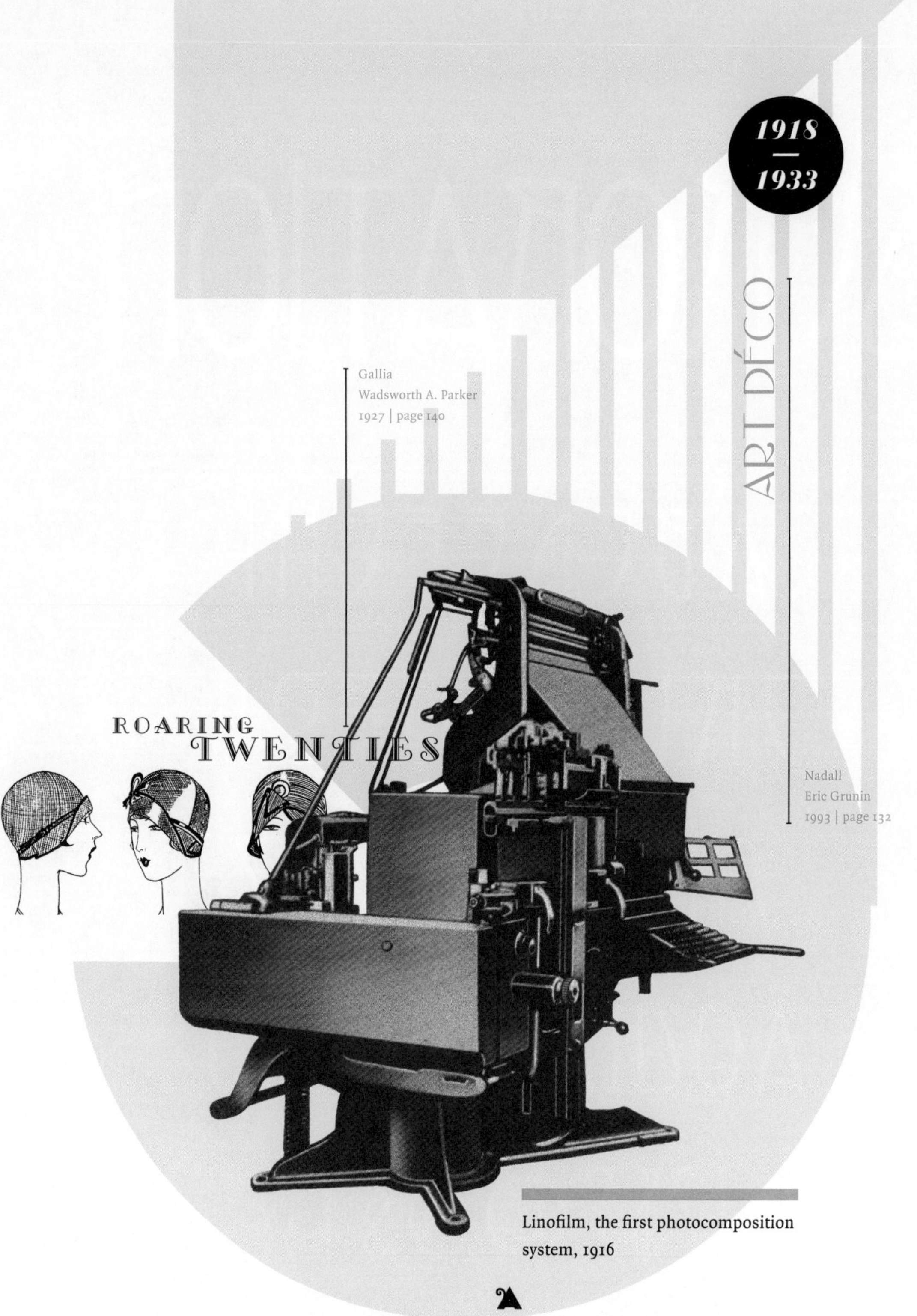

Linofilm, the first photocomposition system, 1916

3 *Cinema, Jazz and Bob Cuts*
Art Deco and Plakatstil

c. 1918–1933

Today the twenties are longingly referred to as the 'roaring twenties' and are inextricably bound up with jazz, swing and celebrities such as Marlene Dietrich and Josephine Baker. Design developed in different but parallel directions, one of which is known as Art Deco. This stylistic period, permanently tied to consumption and elegance, left its mark on typography as well. It focused on finding the ideal form of entertainment and amusement, passing itself off as a representative of the modern Zeitgeist and cultivating the new achievements of the time, including cinema, the gramophone and the telephone.

Vogue
Magazine cover, 1925

Cinema, Jazz and Bob Cuts
Art Deco and Plakatstil

c. 1918–1933

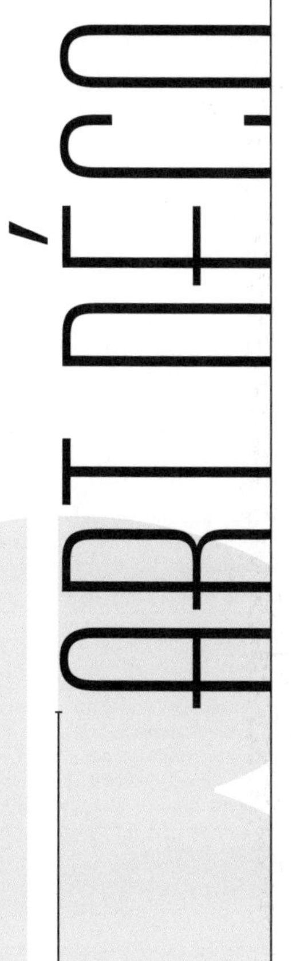

Huxley Vertical
Walter Huxley
1935 | page 152

Art Deco style is based on the geometric formal language of the Constructivists, though it, too, falls prey to a decorative impulse that develops into a love for elegance. This is true also for type design, which, though based on geometry, abstraction and elementary forms, bows in the end to graphic necessity.

Typical Art Deco alphabets have strong, almost unbalanced stroke contrasts, and recall the classical typographical creations. Their change in appearance from narrow to wide is characteristic.

Many typefaces are composed of geometric forms. Visually, they seem flat and ornamental, often at the expense of legibility, and their appearance in poster art is remarkable for this. Frequently, letters receive additional spatial and graphic embellishments.

Along with these emerge countless sans-serif variants of Antique. At times, lowercase letters are completely rejected in favour of capital letters with thin, strong strokes, some of which are excessive in their design. One repeatedly finds in these alphabets a median line that has been shifted higher or lower. These tend also to be justified to the right. Some alphabets are distinguished through stark internal contrasts in letter width. In such cases, uppercase 'S,' 'P' and 'R' can turn out to be very narrow but very wide in relation to rounded forms like the uppercase 'O,' or even 'G' and 'C.'

Typefaces

Constructed decorative typescript

Broadway

Characteristics

Many Art Deco typefaces exhibit extreme contrasts in their body strokes. Even if less severe than classical Antique, they are none the less comparable.

Constructed with classical character

Parisian

Characteristics

The variants of Antique in this era are frequently characterized by a low x-height and a shift in the median line. However, the basic forms resemble their historical paradigms.

Variants of Antiqua

HUXLEY VERTICAL

Characteristics

In the case of sans-serif variants on Antique it is not uncommon to find a median line that has been shifted higher or lower, justified to the right in several alphabetic forms. Often the scripts consist only of uppercase letters.

Sans-serif variants of Antiqua

BIFUR

Characteristics

The constructed decorative typefaces of Art Deco are put together in a purely geometric fashion, often stylized into abstract ornaments. They are characteristically technical, modern and flat.

Characteristics

Example: Broadway Morris Fuller Benton 1925 | page 135

Example: Parisian Morris Fuller Benton 1928 | page 155

Example: Huxley Vertical Walter Huxley 1935 | page 152

Example: Bifur Tomoyuki Watanabe 2002 | page 167

Typefaces

Constructed with classical character and sans-serif variants of Antique, very light styles and all-caps are frequently found in advertising, packaging and newspaper design. Only rarely are sans-serif scripts used as a regular typeface. Antique and fractured scripts remain the standard despite the era's prevailing tastes.

Illustration and Typography

Art Deco illustrations are provocative representations influenced by Cubism. At times they were the mouthpiece of twenties modernism, with its technology, communication, transportation and its dynamism; at other times, of mundane elegance and luxury transposed into a fantastical world of unadulterated glamour that takes precedence over typography. The typography is often muted and modest, giving the visual motif the space and prominence it needs.

Ornaments

Ornaments are motifs composed of geometric designs, sometimes floral, figurative or even abstract. Exemplars can be found in the art of the time, but also in the graphic language of exotic cultures, embodying themes of modern technology and ways of life.

NADALL

60 pt

ABCDEFGHI
JKLMNOPQR
STUVWXYZ
ABCDEFGHIJKLM
NOPQRSTUVWXYZ
ÄÖÜ1234567890
(&ß!?$)

48 pt

Nadall
Eric Grunin, 1993
www.dafont.com

CD

ITC VINTAGE

ILLUSTRIRTE

75 pt

ABCDEFGHI
JKLMNOPQR
STUVWXYZ

ABCDEFGHIJKLM
NOPQRSTUVWXYZ
1234567890
(ÄÖÜ&!?$£€)

43 pt

ITC Vintage
Holly Goldsmith, 1996
www.linotype.com

The Broadway Series
Type sample
American Type Founders, 1925

BROADWAY

Play house

80 pt

ABCDEFGHI
JKLMNOPQRST
UVWXYZ
abcdefghijklm
nopqrstuvwxyz
äöü1234567890
("&ß!?$:;')

35 pt

Broadway
Morris Fuller Benton, 1925
www.linotype.com

EMPIRE STATE DECO

EMPIRE

90 pt

ABCDEFGHI
JKLMNOPQRST
UVWXYZ
ABCDEFGHI
JKLMNOPQRST
UVWXYZ
1234567890

FULLTILTBOOGIE

SPIELBANK

65 pt

ABCDEFGHI

JKLMNOPQR

STUVWXYZ

1234567890

&!?$£€*

50 pt

FullTiltBoogie
Nick Curtis, 1999
www.nicksfonts.com

CD

BERNHARD FASHION

130 pt

ABCDEFGHI
JKLMNOPQR
STUVWXYZ
abcdefghijklm
nopqrstuvwxyzäöü
1234567890
(„&fiflß!?$£:;*")

40 pt

Bernhard Fashion
Lucian Bernhard, 1929
www.linotype.com

Seida
Wine label
Louise Fili Ltd, c. 2000

GALLIA

TOPF-
HUT

85 pt

A A B B C D E E F G
H I J K L L M M
N O P Q R R S S T T
U V V W W X X
Y Y Z Z Ä Ö Ü
1 2 3 4 5 6 7 8 9 0
(& ! ? $ £ € @ : ;)

40 pt

Gallia
Wadsworth A. Parker, 1927
www.linotype.com

METRO-RETRO

ROBE

115 pt

ABCDEFGHI

JKLMNOPQR

STUVWXYZ

1234567890

„&!?$£€“

50 pt

Metro-Retro
Nick Curtis, 1999
www.nicksfonts.com

CD

LABYRINTH

105 pt

ABCDEFG
HIJKLM
NOPQRST
UVWXYZ
1234567890
„&!?ÄÖÜ“

55 pt

Labyrinth
Nick Curtis, 1999
www.nicksfonts.com

CD

Dolce & Gabbana,
Website, 2008

GUINNESSEXTRASTOUT

Fine jewelry
French cabinet
Music
Wallpaper

20 pt

ABCDEFGHI
JKLMNOPQR
STUVWXYZ
abcdefghijklm
nopqrstuvwxyz
äöü1234567890
(»&ﬁß!?$£€©®*«)

30 pt

GuinnessExtraStout
Nick Curtis, 1999
www.nicksfonts.com

CD

FONTLEROYBROWN

Tobacco

150 pt

A B C D E F G H I
J K L M N O P Q R
S T U V W X Y Z
a b c d e f g h i j k l m
n o p q r s t u v w x y z ä ö ü
1 2 3 4 5 6 7 8 9 0
(& ! ? $ £ €)

48 pt

FontleroyBrown
Nick Curtis, 2000
www.dafont.com

CD

Vogue
Advertisement
F. Wolff & Sohn, 1923

PLATONICK-NORMAL

AUTOMOBIL

125 pt

ABCDEFGHI
JKLMNOPQRST
UVWXYZÄÖÜ
1234567890
{([&ß!?$£€*])}

55 pt

Platonick-Normal
Nick Curtis, 1997
www.nicksfonts.com

CD

ANAKRONISM

Parfüm

Creme, Puder und Seife

60 / 20 pt

A B C D E F G H I

J K L M N O P Q R

S T U V W X Y Z

a b c d e f g h i j k l m

n o p q r s t u v w x y z ä ö ü

1 2 3 4 5 6 7 8 9 0

& ß ! ? $ £ € †

35 pt

AnAkronism
Nick Curtis, 1999
www.dafont.com

CD

ANTIQUE NO 14

Schuhcreme

60 pt

ABCDEFGHI
JKLMNOPQR
STUVWXYZ
abcdefghijklm
nopqrstuvwxyz
äöü1234567890
(&!?$@)

35 pt

Antique No 14
Dieter Steffmann, 2000
www.steffmann.de

[illegible] CD

Propaganda
Book cover
Politzer, c. 1930

UNCLE BOB MF

PRALINE

75 pt

ABCDEFGHIJ

KLMNOPQRST

UVWXYZÄÖÜ

1234567890

(&!?$Ł)

40 pt

Uncle Bob MF
Richard William Mueller, 1993
moorstation.org/typoasis/designers/mueller

☞ CD

HUXLEY VERTICAL

HERMES

180 pt

ABCDEFGHIJK

LMNOPQRST

UVWXYZ

1234567890

(&!?$£†)

70 pt

Huxley Vertical
Walter Huxley, 1935
www.bitstream.com

Rockefeller Center
Logo
Doyle Partners, c. 2000

PEIGNOT

Plakat
wand

85 pt

ABCDEFGHI
JKLMNOPQR
STUVWXYZ
abcdefghijklm
nopqrstuvwxyzäöü
1234567890
(&ß!?$@)

44 pt

Peignot
A. M. Cassandre, 1937
www.linotype.com

PARISIAN

Golden Twenties

70 pt

ABCDEFGHI
JKLMNOPQR
STUVWXYZ
abcdefghijklm
nopqrstuvwxyzäöü
1234567890
(&ß!?$†)

40 pt

Parisian
Morris Fuller Benton, 1928
www.linotype.com

THE LEGS OF THE
STORK ARE LONG-
THE LEGS OF THE
DUCK ARE SHORT
---YOU CANNOT
MAKE THE LEGS
OF THE STORK
SHORT-NEITHER
CAN YOU MAKE
THE LEGS OF THE
DUCK LONG-

WHY WORRY?

Why Worry?
Book cover, 1932

BREMEN

THE LEGS OF THE STORK

35 / 90 pt

ABCDEFGH
IJKLMNO
PQRSTUVW
XYZÄÖÜ
1234567890
(„&!?$†:;")

42 pt

Bremen
Richard Lipton, 1990-92
after Ludwig Holhlwein, 1922
www.bitstream.com

ODALISQUE

FINANZ
ADEL

80 pt

ABCDEFGHI
JKLMNOPQR
STUVWXYZ
1234567890
(&!?ÄÖÜ$£€)

50 pt

Odalisque
Nick Curtis, 2000
www.nicksfonts.com

CD

SARSAPARILLA

Fashion

110 pt

ABCDEFGHI
JKLMNOPQRST
UVWXYZ
abcdefghijklm
nopqrstuvwxyz
äöü1234567890
&ß!?$£€

46 pt

DRUMAGSTUDIONF

BAR

150 pt

ABCDEFGHIJ

KLMNOPQRST

UVWXZÄÖÜ

1234567890

(„&! $£€@")

38 pt

DrumagStudioNF
Nick Curtis, 2003
www.nicksfonts.com

Stone's Throw
Wine label
Morrow McKenzie Design, 2000

XYLO

Freitag

95 pt

ABCDEFGHI
JKLMNOPQR
STUVWXYZ
abcdefghijklm
nopqrstuvwxyz
1234567890
(äöü&ß!?$£€:;)

43 pt

Xylo
Benjamin Krebs, 1924
www.linotype.com

DOLMEN

Average

85 pt

ABCDEFGHI
JKLMNOPQR
STUVWXYZ
abcdefghijklm
nopqrstuvwxyz
1234567890
(äöü&ß!?$£€)

42 pt

Dolmen
Max Salzmann, 1922
www.linotype.com

Vogue
Magazine cover, 1929

COPASETIC

THEATER

115 pt

ABCDEFGHIJKLMN
OPQRSTUVWXYZÄÖÜ
ABCDEFGHIJKLM
N°PQRSTUVWXYZÄ°Ü
1234567890
»&ß!?$£€ÆÆŒ«

43 pt

Copasetic
Nick Curtis, 1999
www.nicksfonts.com

CD

BRADLEY INITIALS

DR.
CALIGARI

60 pt

ABCDEFGHIJKLM

NOPQRSTUVWXYZ

ABCDEFGHIJKLM

NOPQRSTUVWXYZ

1234567890

&$€:;

29 pt

Bradley Initials
William H. Bradley, 1934
www.fontbureau.com

BIFUR

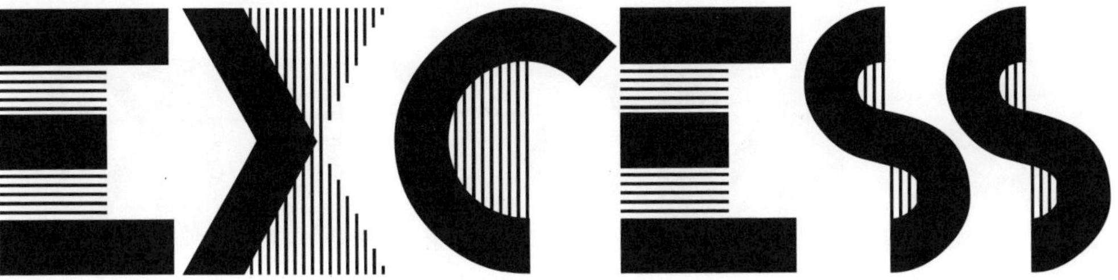

110 pt

ABCDEFGHIJ
KLMNOPQRST
UVWXYZ
1234567890
(‹!?&›)

49 pt

Bifur
Tomoyuki Watanabe, 2002
A. J. M. Cassandre, 1927
typography.jp.org

CD

FANCYPANTS

ANTIK

90 pt

ABCDEFGHIJKLM
NOPQRSTUVWXYZ
ABCDEFGHIJKL
MNOPQRSTU
VWXYZ
1234567890
»&ß!?ÄÖÜ£$€*:;«

34 pt

FancyPants
Nick Curtis, 1999
www.nicksfonts.com

☞ CD

Dom Perignon
Poster
Terry Allen, c. 2000

METROPOLIS CT

Josephine Baker

75 pt

ABCDEFGHI
JKLMNOPQR
STUVWXYZ
abcdefghijklm
nopqrstuvwxyz
1234567890
(äöü&ß!?$:;)

41 pt

Metropolis CT
Jason Castle, 1990
W. Schwerdtner, 1932
www.castletype.com

MODERNIQUE

Striptease

80 pt

ABCDEFGHI
JKLMNOPQR
STUVWXYZ
abcdefghijklm
nopqrstuvwxyz
äöü1234567890
★(&ß!?$£)☆

40 pt

ANAGRAM

METRO

95 pt

ABCDEFG
HIJKLMNOP
QRSTUV
WXYZÄÖÜ
1234567890
„&ß!?$£€:;"

48 pt

Anagram
Nick Curtis, 1999
www.nicksfonts.com

☞ CD

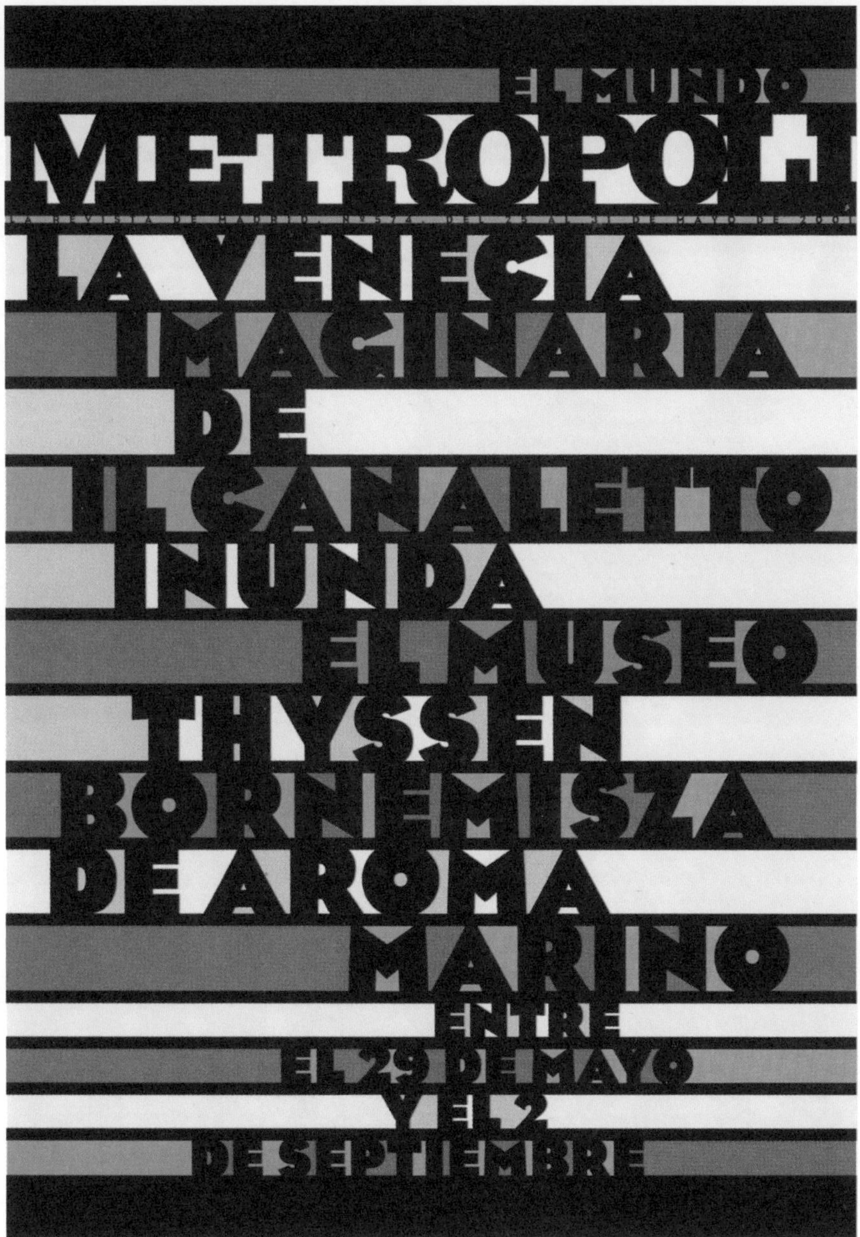

El Mundo Metropoli
Magazine cover
Unidad Editorial S.A., 2001

SUNSET

Seehaus

150 pt

ABCDEFGHI
JKLMNOPQR
STUVWXYZ
abcdefghijklm
nopqrstuvwxyz
äöü1234567890
(&ß!?$£€@☮)

48 pt

Sunset
Harold Lohner, 2004
www.haroldsfonts.com

CD

DHARMA

Strand

110 pt

ABCDEFGHI
JKLMNOPQR
STUVWXYZ
abcdefghijklm
nopqrstuvwxyz
1234567890
(äöü&ß!?$€@)

42 pt

Dharma
Gerd Sebastian Jakob, 1997
Joerg Ewald Meißner, 1922
www.linotype.com

BINNER GOTHIC

Kaffeehaus

145 pt

ABCDEFGHIJKLM
NOPQRSTUVWXYZ
abcdefghijklm
nopqrstuvwxyzäöü
1234567890
(„&fiflß!?$£@“)

50 pt

Binner Gothic
John F. Cummings, 1898
www.linotype.com

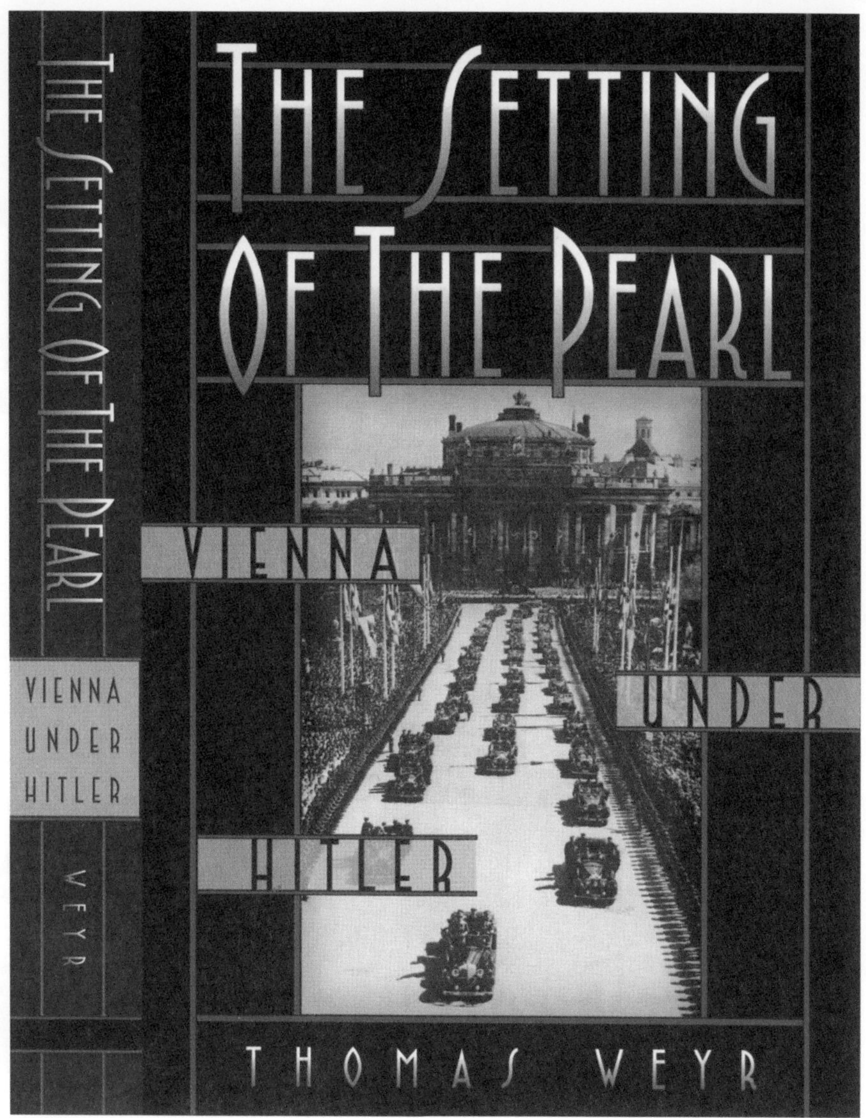

The Setting of the Pearl
Book cover
Jon Valk Design, 2005

FACETSNF

CASINO

120 pt

ABCDEFGHI

JKLMNOPQRST

UVWXYZÄÖÜ

1234567890

»(&!?$£€@)«

60 pt

FacetsNF
Nick Curtis, 2003
www.dafont.com

CD

POPUPS

THE
METRO
STATION

60 pt

ABCDEFGHI
JKLMNOPQR
STUVWXYZ
A B C D E F G H I J K L M
N O P Q R S T U V W X Y Z
1234567890
THE AND TO WITH IN BY FOR

45 pt

PopUps
Harold Lohner, 1998
www.haroldsfonts.com

☞ CD

Europe at Love
Book cover
Hans Flato, 1932

NICKELODEON

Limited Edition

84 pt

ABCDEFGHI
JKLMNOPQRST
UVWXYZ
abcdefghijklm
nopqrstuvwxyz
äöü1234567890
(&ß!?$€)

50 pt

Nickelodeon
Nick Curtis, 1999
www.nicksfonts.com

CD

BEAUTYSCHOOLDROPOUT II

OLDTIMER

145 pt

ABCDEFGHIJKLM

NOPQRSTUVWXYZ

ABCDEFGHIJKLMN

OPQRSTUVWXYZÄÖÜ

1234567890

(&ß!?$£€@)

45 pt

BeautySchoolDropout II
Nick Curtis, 1997, 2000
www.dafont.com

☞ CD

SHOWTIME

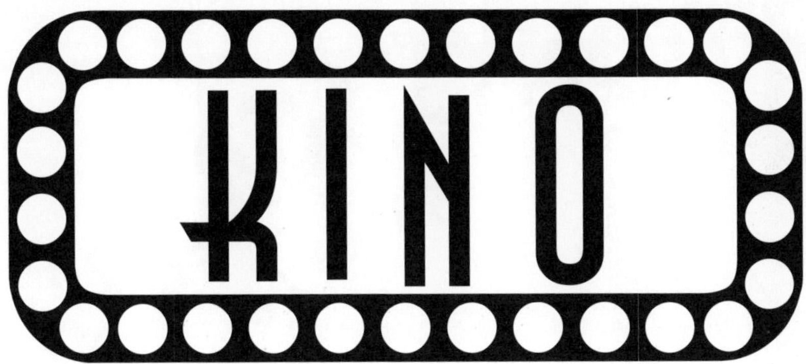

100 pt

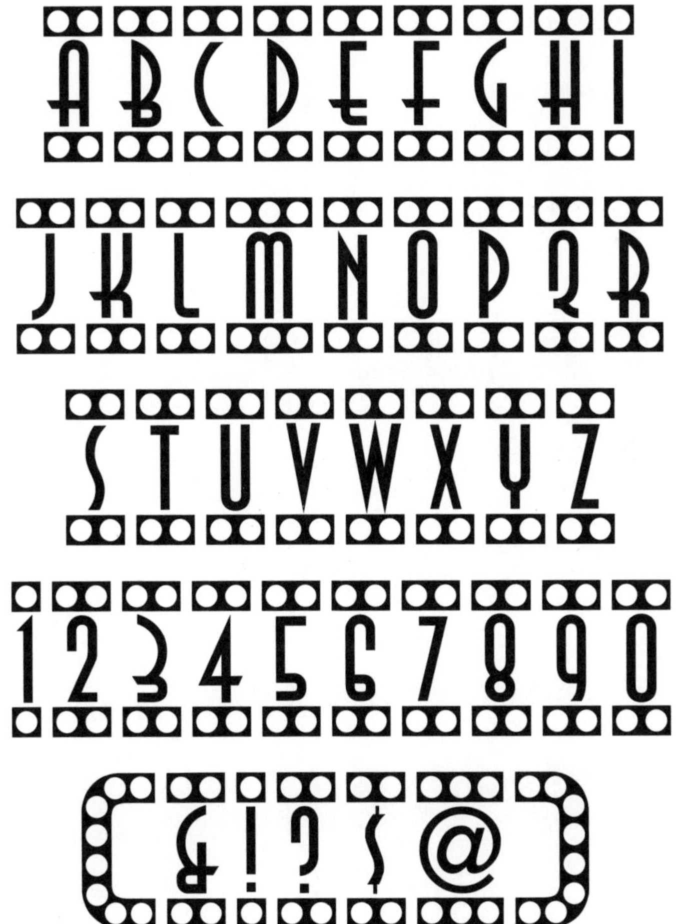

45 pt

Showtime
Randy Ford, 1998
fonts.arrfdesigns.com

CD

TONY'S SCRAP BOOK

1932-33 EDITION

by
Tony Wons

Tony's Scrap Book
Book cover, 1933

FIESTA

SILBER

150 pt

ABCDEFGHIJ
KLMNOPQRST
UVWXYZ
1234567890

58 pt

Fiesta
Bartek Nowak, 2001
www.nowak.tv/fontoholic

CD

UMBRA

AVENUE

100 pt

ABCDEFG
HIJKLMNOP
QRSTUV
WXYZÄÖÜ
1234567890
„&!?$£†*:;"

50 pt

Umbra
Robert Hunter Middleton, 1932
www.linotype.com

Fate
Poster
Joe Scorsone, Alice Drueding, 1997

ZEPPELIN

Zylinder

120 pt

ABCDEFGHI
JKLMNOPQR
STUVWXYZ
abcdefghijklm
nopqrstuvwxyz
äöü1234567890
(&fiflß!?$£)

45 pt

Zeppelin
Rudolf Koch, 1927
www.linotype.com

Breuninger
Book cover
Mutabor Design, 2006

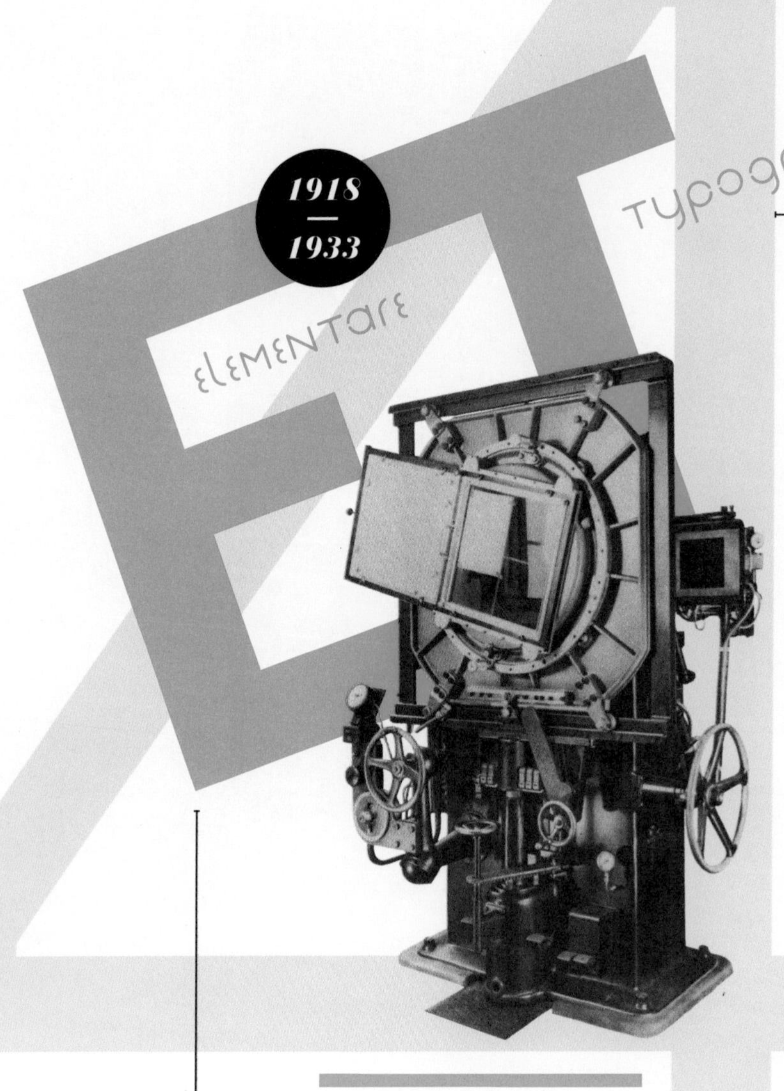

Das Reicht Gut
Matt Perkins
1997 | page 216

Uhertype photo-typesetting machine, 1930

Futura
Paul Renner
1928 | page 196

E

4 *Tschichold and Bauhaus Elementary Typography and Constructivism*

c. 1918–1933

Elementary Typography developed in Germany at the same time as the inception of Art Deco design, in the period between the end of World War I and the rise to power of the National Socialists. There were many forerunners of the 'new typography'. The Constructivists, Dadaists and Futurists, with their bold typographical compositions, were the forefathers of certain formal attempts at Elementary Typography.

Sportpolitische Rundschau
Magazine cover
Jan Tschichold, 1928

Tschichold and Bauhaus Elementary Typography and Constructivism

c. 1918–1933

DIN Mittelschrift
Ludwig Goller
1925 | page 202

Tschich
Manfred Klein
2002 | page 201

TYPOGRAFIE

The traditional typefaces, Antique and Fraktur, were no longer perceived as contemporary. It was argued that elementary forms – circles, squares and triangles, for example – were better suited to modern life. Formal concerns had immediate influence on type design. Corresponding alphabets were constructed by assembling exclusively circular, triangular and rectangular elements. Because the slight differences between individual letters are indiscernible without isolating their elements, these alphabets resemble stencilled scripts.

At the same time the so-called 'Universal' alphabets emerged, based on the belief that both large and small signs are not necessary to indicate a single sound, so therefore a single alphabet would be sufficient. Thus, experimental alphabets were developed based on lowercase letters only. Though uppercase letters are, as a rule, only rarely encountered, when they do appear it is a result of either direct assimilation or hybrid mutation. On account of their poor legibility, however, these scripts could not be used for body text.

The Grotesque typefaces are perfectly legible and timeless, and indeed they seem to have been constructed with a compass and ruler. They weren't, of course, but they were graphically amended in the interest of improved legibility, and it was just this kind of respect for the optical laws of better legibility that probably brought the famous Futura into existence.

Typefaces

Sans-serif scripts with an artificially constructed character

Charactertisitcs

Futura

Although in this species of script the basic geometrical forms are still recognizable, the construction has returned to a concern for the overall appearance and its legibility.

Sans-serif scripts

Charactertisitcs

P22 Albers

Typical Bauhaus scripts are assembled exclusively from circular, triangular or rectangular elements.

Stenciled scripts

Charactertisitcs

tschich

Universal scripts were usually based on lowercase letters. Many letters are even a hybrid form of uppercase and lowercase. These scripts are severe in their construction.

Universal scripts

Charactertisitcs

Kabel

A sans-serif based on geometric shapes. Its bas forms were influenced by the Roman Capitalis, which also consisted of just a few, clear geometric forms – circle, square and triangle. The x-height is small and character widths variable, making it most suitable for display setting.

Charactertisitcs

Example:
Futura
Paul Renner
1928 | page 196

Example:
P22 Albers
Richard Kegler
2007 | page 220

Example:
Tschich
Manfred Klein
2002 | page 201

Example:
Kabel
Rudolf Koch
1925 | page 197

Typefaces

The exclusive use of sans-serif typefaces is the rule, although these may come in any of the available styles – thin or thick, narrow or wide. In the beginning, the sans-serif fonts available prior to the twenties were still in use (mostly commercial Grotesque, Venus and News Gothic) but the later years saw the design of highly constructed and stencilled scripts.

Text

Centred text is superseded by block and unjustified text. This saved the typesetter time and has a more natural appearance since it is not oriented on an axis. This comes at greater cost to the relationship between image and background, and white space is now integrated into the design. The free composition of typographical elements and diagonal text is also modern.

Ornaments

Historical detail is superseded by elementary forms (circles, triangles and rectangles) and lines. Their use is governed by the construction of the whole. Special attention is given to designs that incorporate stark contrasts, though their importance must be determined by their relation to content.

FUTURA

Zu den elementaren Mitteln der Typographie gehört in der heutigen, auf Optik eingestellten Welt auch das exakte Bild:

die Photographie

15 / 48 pt

ABCDEFGHI
JKLMNOPQR
STUVWXYZ
abcdefghijklm
nopqrstuvwxyz
1234567890
(äöü!?&ß$£)

38 pt

Futura
Paul Renner, 1928
www.linotype.com

KABEL

Elementare Schriftform
ist die Groteskschrift
aller Variationen

40 pt

ABCDEFGHI
JKLMNOPQR
STUVWXYZ
abcdefghijklm
nopqrstuvwxyz
1234567890
(äöü!?&ßfifl$£)

38 pt

Kabel
Rudolf Koch, 1925
www.linotype.com

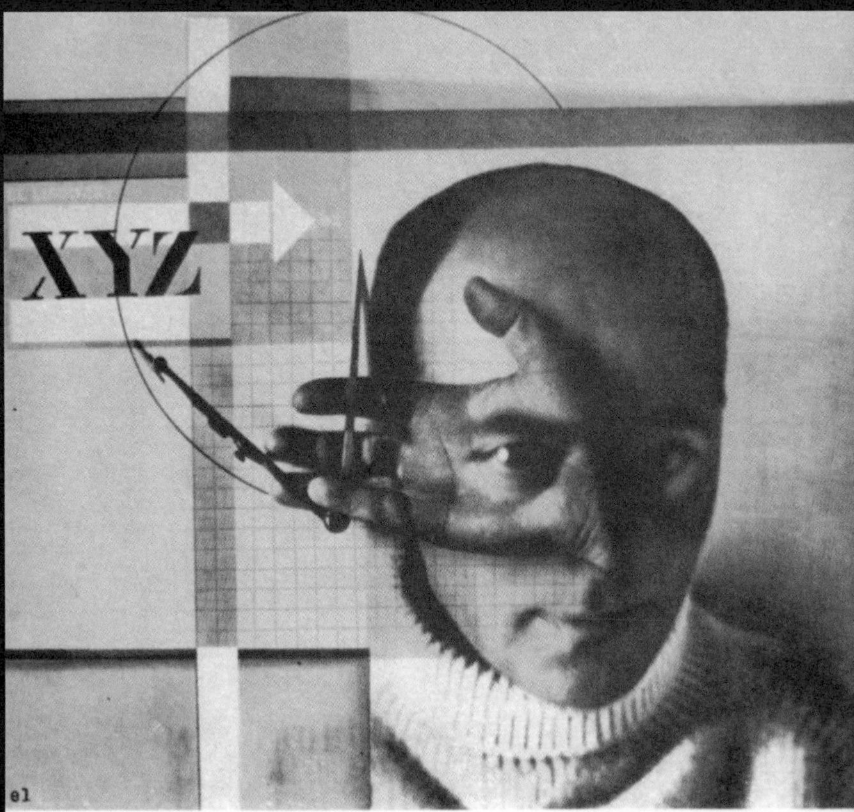

Photo-eye
Magazine cover
Jan Tschichold, 1928

ERBAR

Es wäre zum mindesten unproduktiver Zeitverlust, wenn man heute beweisen wollte, dass man nicht mit eigenem Blut und einer Gänsefeder zu schreiben braucht, wenn die Schreibmaschine existiert. Heute zu beweisen, dass die Aufgabe jedes Schaffens, so auch der Kunst, nicht DARstellen, sondern DAstellen ist, ist ebenfalls unproduktiver Zeitverlust.

15 pt

A B C D E F G H I
J K L M N O P Q R
S T U V W X Y Z
a b c d e f g h i j k l m
n o p q r s t u v w x y z
1 2 3 4 5 6 7 8 9 0
(ä ö ü & ! ? $ £ @)

40 pt

Erbar
Jakob Erbar, 1930
www.linotype.com

GEO SANS LIGHT

Schriften, die bestimmten Stilarten angehören oder beschränkt-nationalen Charakter tragen, sind nicht elementar gestaltet und beschränken zum Teil die internationale Verständigungsmöglichkeit.

20 pt

ABCDEFGHI
JKLMNOPQR
STUVWXYZ
abcdefghijklm
nopqrstuvwxyz
äöü1234567890
(!?&ftß$£€)

40 pt

Geo Sans Light
Manfred Klein, 2003
www.moorstation.org/typoasis/designers/klein

☞ CD

TSCHICH

vir dürfen niht fergesen, das vir an ainer vende der kultur stehen, am ende ales alten

30 pt

abcdefghi
jklmnopqr
stuvwxyz
wzäöü
1234567890
(!?&ßssss€)

50 pt

Tschich
Manfred Klein, 2002
www.moorstation.org/typoasis/designers/klein

CD

DIN MITTELSCHRIFT

Zweck jeder Typographie ist Mitteilung.

Die Mitteilung muss in kürzester, einfachster,

eindringlichster Form erscheinen.

18 pt

ABCDEFGHI
JKLMNOPQR
STUVWXYZ
abcdefghijklm
nopqrstuvwxyz
1234567890
(äöü&fiflß$£)

40 pt

DIN Mittelschrift
Ludwig Goller, 1925
www.linotype.com

Misalliance
Poster
Sandstorm Design, 2006

IWAN RESCHNIEV

Tschichold

110 pt

A B C D E F G H I
J K L M N O P Q R
S T U V W X Y Z
a b c d e f g h i j k l m
n o p q r s ſ t u v w x y z
ä ö ü 1 2 3 4 5 6 7 8 9 0
(! ¡ ? & ẞ ß $ £ € @)

45 pt

Iwan Reschniev
Sebastian Nagel, 2008
Jan Tschichold, 1930
www.fonts.info

P22 CONSTRUCTIVIST

ARCHITEKT

60 pt

ABCDEF
GHIJKL
MNOPQR
STUVW
XYZÄÖÜ
1234567890
(!?&ß$€@)

49 pt

P22 Constructivist
Richard Kegler, 2007
www.p22.com

P22 BAYER UNIVERSAL

ring neuer
werbegestalter

60 pt

a b c d e f g
h i j k l m n o
p q r s t u v
w x y z ä ö ü
1 2 3 4 5 6 7 8 9 0
(! ? & ß $ £ € @)

55 pt

P22 Bayer Universal
Denis Kegler, Richard Kegler, 2007
Herbert Bayer, 1925
www.p22.com

The Insanity of normality
Book cover
Carin Goldberg, 1992

MAMMA GAMMA

less is **more**

80 pt

abcdefghi
jklmnopqr
stuvwxyz

abcdefghijklm
nopqrstuvwxyz
1234567890
(!?&@)

44 pt

Mamma Gamma
Jakob Fischer, 2003
www.pizzadude.dk

☞ CD

MODERNA

Collage

100 pt

ABCDEFGHI
JKLMNOPQR
STUVWXYZ
abcdefghijklm
nopqrstuvwxyz
"/!:·.

38 pt

Moderna
Fontalicious Fonts, 2002
www.fontalicious.com

CD

Der General
Poster
Jan Tschichold, 1927

BANK GOTHIC

HELDEN DER
LEINWAND

30 / 80 pt

ABCDEFGHI
JKLMNOPQRS
TUVWXYZÄÖÜ
ABCDEFGHIJKLM
NOPQRSTUVWXYZ
1234567890
(&!?$£€:;*)

48 pt

Bank Gothic
Morris Fuller Benton, 1930
www.bitstream.com

GILL SANS

Innere Organisation ist Beschränkung auf die elementaren Mittel der Typographie: Schrift, Zahlen, Zeichen, Linien des Setzkastens und der Setzmaschine.

15 pt

ABCDEFGHI
JKLMNOPQR
STUVWXYZ
abcdefghijklm
nopqrstuvwxyz
1234567890
(äöü!?&ßfifl$£€)

43 pt

Gill Sans
Eric Gill, 1929
www.linotype.com

NOBEL

Amsterdam

85 pt

ABCDEFGHI
JKLMNOPQR
STUVWXYZ
abcdefghijklm
nopqrstuvwxyz
1234567890
(äöü!?&ß$£€@)

41 pt

Nobel
Fred Smeijers, 1992
Sjoerd Henrik de Roos, 1930
www.fontbureau.com

GOCA LOGOTYPE BETA

FLYER

110 pt

ABCDEFGH
IJKLMNO
PQRSTUV
WXYZ
1234567890
»!?®©@«

50 pt

Goca Logotype Beta
Jonas Borneland Hansen, 2008
www.dafont.com

CD

Southern Sessions,
Flyer, C100 Purple Haze, 2006

DAS REICHT GUT

tsu jedem tsaitpunkt der
ferganenhait varen ale
variatsjonen des alten noi

30 pt

abcdefghi
jklmnopqr
stuvwxyz
1234567890
, ! ? ' :

65 pt

Das Reicht Gut
Matt Perkins, 1997
Jan Tschichold, 1929
www.dafont.com

CD

DIN SCHABLONIERSCHRIFT

GEHEIM!

115 pt

ABCDEFGHI

JKLMNOPQR

STUVWXYZ

1234567890

&!:;

58 pt

DIN Schablonierschrift
Marian Steinbach, 2004
www.dafont.com

CD

ARMIN

METALL

130 pt

ABCDEFGHI

JKLMNOPQR

STUVWXYZ

1234567890

"&?$'

55 pt

Armin
Romuald Kowalczyk, 2005
www.dafont.com

☞ CD

BD ALM

KOMBI
NATION

59 pt

abcdefghi
jklmnopqr
stuvwxyz
1234567890
("&!?#¥)

46 pt

BD Alm
Büro Destruct, 2001
www.typedifferent.com

☞ CD

P22 ALBERS

Metallglas

90 pt

A B C D E F G H I

J K L M N O P Q R

S T U V W X Y Z

a b c d e f g h i j k l m

n o p q r s t u v w x y z

ä ö ü 1 2 3 4 5 6 7 8 9 0

(! ? & ſ * $ £ € @)

43 pt

P22 Albers
Richard Kegler, 2007
Josef Albers, 1923
www.p22.com

NYAMOMOBILE

stahlrohr

95 pt

abcdefghi

jklmnopqr

stuvwxyz

1234567890

äöü

55 pt

Nyamomobile
Vic Fieger, 2006
www.vicfieger.com

☞ CD

Laster der Menschheit
Poster
Jan Tschichold, 1927

BIGNOODLETITLING

LASTER

175 pt

ABCDEFGHI
JKLMNOPQR
STUVWXYZ
ÄÖÜFIFL
1234567890
(&!?$£€@)

50 pt

BigNoodleTitling
James Arboghast, 2003
www.dafont.com

☞ CD

FUTURA LT BLACK

Meisterschule
für Deutschlands Buchdrucker

65 / 30 pt

ABCDEFGHI
JKLMNOPQR
STUVWXYZ
abcdefghijklm
nopqrstuvwxyz
1234567890
(äöü!?&ß$£€@)

43 pt

Futura LT Black
Paul Renner, 1928
www.linotype.com

LAMIA

qualle

110 pt

a b c d e f g

h i j k l m n

o p q r s t u

v w x y z

1 2 3 4 5 6

7 8 9 0

48 pt

Lamia
Benoît Sjöholm, 2008
www.calamedesign.com

☞ CD

STUNTMAN

110 pt

ABCDEFGHIJKLM

NOPQRSTUVWXYZ

abcdefghijklm

nopqrstuvwxyz

1234567890

(äöüß!?$€@)

35 pt

Stuntman
Daniel Zadorozny, 2003
www.iconian.com

☞ CD

Academy of Fine Arts Lodz
Poster
Jakub Stepien, 2003

AVENGER

100 pt

abcdefghi
jklmnopqr
stuvwxyz
ABCDEFGHI
JKLMNOPQR
STUVWXYZ
1234567890

40 pt

Avenger
Daniel Zadorozny, 2008
www.iconian.com

CD

DEPTHCORE PUBLIC

105 pt

abcdef
ghijk
lmnopqr
stuvw
xyz
123456
7890

60 pt

Depthcore Public
Rob Janssen, 2002
www.dafont.com

☞ CD

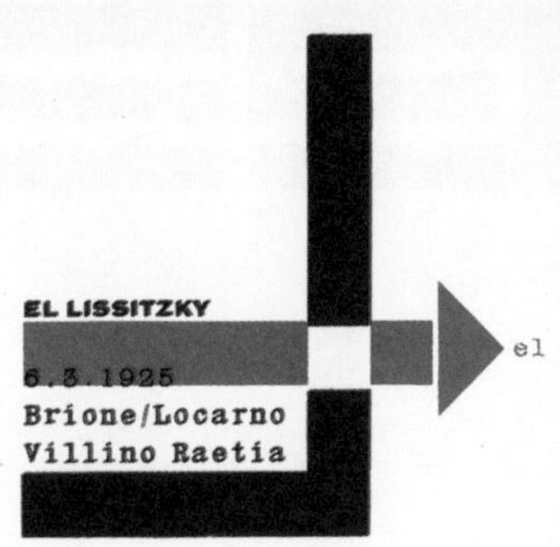

EL LISSITZKY

6.3.1925
Brione/Locarno
Villino Raetia

el

IWAN TSCHICHOLD
LEIPZIG

Es wäre zum mindesten unproduktiver Zeitverlust, wenn man heute beweisen wollte, dass man nicht mit eigenem Blut und einer Gänsefeder zu schreiben braucht, wenn die Schreibmaschine existiert. Heute zu beweisen, dass die Aufgabe jedes Schaffens, so auch der Kunst, nicht DARstellen, sondern DAstellen ist, ist ebenfalls unproduktiver Zeitverlust. (Merz)

El Lissitzky

Letterhead
El Lissitzky, 1925

TURNPIKE

BRIEF

85 pt

ABCDEF
GHIJK
LMNOPQ
RSTUV
WXYZÄÖÜ
1234567890
(„&!?$£€")

40 pt

Turnpike
Font Diner, 2008
www.fontdiner.com

CD

FUTURA CLASSIC

Alternative Figuren zeichnen diese Schrift aus

50 / 36 pt

ABCDEFGHI
JKLMNOPQR
STUVWXYZ
abcdefghijklm
nopqrstuvwxyz
äöü1234567890
(!?&fiflffftfftß$€@)

38 pt

Futura Classic
Gert Wiescher, 2006
Paul Renner, 1928
www.wiescher-design.de

SPEEDLEARN

UNSUMME

95 pt

ABCDEFGHI
JKLMNOPQR
STUVWXYZ
ABCDEFGHIJKLM
NOPQRSTUVWXYZ
1234567890
ÄÖÜ!€:;

45 pt

Speedlearn
SDFonts, 2001
jump.to/sdfonts

☞ CD

Traditionsverbundene Typografie

1933 — 1945

Tannenberg Fett
Dieter Steffmann
2002 | page 258

Nationalsozialismus

Fette Trump-D
Dieter Steffma
2002 | page 25

First electric typewriter, IBM, 1933

D

5 Cult of Personality and Popular Reception
The Typography of Tradition

c. 1933–1945

When the National Socialists came to power in 1933, fractured typefaces were immediately promulgated as authentically 'German' and only a year later were required in all official documents. Nevertheless, the typography of the Third Reich was not as unified as is generally assumed. Its Neoclassical, Monumental architecture is much better accommodated by the roman forms of Antique. This probably explains why the header of the Nazis' propaganda newspaper, *Völkischer Beobachter* (literally, the 'Popular Observer') is set in uppercase roman letters. In addition, progressive typesetters developed a 'New Typography' that at times was even used in official documents.

Luftschutz!
Poster
Ludwig Hohlwein, 1936

Cult of Personality and Popular Reception The Typography of Tradition

c. 1933–1945

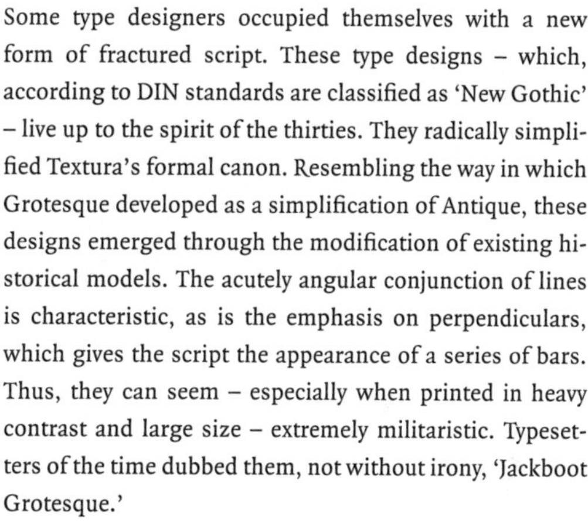

Some type designers occupied themselves with a new form of fractured script. These type designs – which, according to DIN standards are classified as 'New Gothic' – live up to the spirit of the thirties. They radically simplified Textura's formal canon. Resembling the way in which Grotesque developed as a simplification of Antique, these designs emerged through the modification of existing historical models. The acutely angular conjunction of lines is characteristic, as is the emphasis on perpendiculars, which gives the script the appearance of a series of bars. Thus, they can seem – especially when printed in heavy contrast and large size – extremely militaristic. Typesetters of the time dubbed them, not without irony, 'Jackboot Grotesque.'

For years the Nazi Party championed gothic lettering as 'German script,' so that eventually the entire species of these typefaces was known in the collective consciousness as the 'Nazi script.' This despite the fact that Hitler's deputy, Martin Bormann, drafted his secret (but now well known) memorandum of 1941, in which fractured scripts were suddenly demonized as 'Swabian Jew-letters.' Subsequently, authorities permitted the use only of Antique, which was portrayed as the 'normal script.' And although the so-called Normalschrifterlass (literally, 'Decree Regarding Normal Script') did not put in place an official prohibition, it left a mark on the graphic design trade.

Under Nazi dictat and for some time thereafter, sans-serif scripts enjoyed a more prominent role. So, for example, the official typeface of the German Reichsbahn ('Imperial Railroad') became Futura, a font whose creator, Paul Renner, had been branded a cultural bolshevist by the Nazis. Posters for the 1936 Olympic Games featured a similar design.

Typefaces

Sans-serifs scripts

Characteristics

Berthold City

Their forms are based on sans-serif, linear Antique. Visually, all perpendiculars, curves and serifs have the same line widths; hence their robust and stable character.

Linear Antiqua with accentuated serifs

Characteristics

Tannenberg

The New Gothic type designs are considered typical up to 1941. They represent an attempt to abstract the forms of the historical Textura.

New Gothic Scripts

Characteristics

Fette Thannhaeuser

A line of type designs emerged that were in opposition to the attempt to take the fractured scripts beyond their traditional form.

Fraktur

Characteristics

Candida

The classical expression of these variants of Antique did not appeal to contemporary tastes. Most popular in their thick styles, they seem somewhat clumsy.

Variants of Antiqua

Characteristics

SavingsBond

Many sans-serif typefaces of the thirties appear over-large and in many cases crudely constructed. Utterly unsuitable for body text, they allow for narrow and thick styles.

Characteristics

Typefaces

The New Gothic scripts (casually referred to as 'Jackboot Grotesque') were best suited to Nazi propaganda. More than anything else, the simple fractured forms served as display types, as alternatives to different styles of Grotesque and Antique. Fraktur and Schwabascher were mainly used for body text. In the wake of the Normalschrifterlass, designs featuring Antique were ubiquitous, while the use of fractured scripts became less common.

Text and Illustration

Title pages and advertisements were, as a rule centred. Some lines were designed to be powerful, with large font sizes, especially on posters. Woodcuts and watercolours with idealized motifs, were popular in illustrations of the period.

Ornament

Rune-like ornaments, woodcuts and eagles were typical typographical decorations. In addition, the swastika was used in a decorative fashion, for example, built into a border or employed as an embellishment in the corners of documents.

Example:
Berthold City Bold
Georg Trump
1930 | page 241

Example:
Tannenberg Fett
Dieter Steffmann
2002 | page 258

Example:
Fette Thannhaeuser
Dieter Steffmann
2001 | page 252

Example:
Candida Bold
Jakob Erbar
1936 | page 280

Example:
SavingsBond
Harold Lohner
1998 | page 290

Reichs-Gartenschau Stuttgart
Poster, 1939

BERTHOLD CITY BOLD

Spatenstich

80 pt

ABCDEFGHI
JKLMNOPQR
STUVWXYZ
abcdefghijklm
nopqrstuvwxyz
1234567890
äöü&fifl߀$£

40 pt

Berthold City Bold
Georg Trump, 1930
www.bertholdtypes.com

BETON

It consists of a photographic reproduction camera, which carries on a glass disc, measuring 27 x 33 cm, the characters being dealt with at the time, and projects them for setting-up in any suitable size on 35 mm film strip.

15 pt

ABCDEFGHI
JKLMNOPQR
STUVWXYZ
abcdefghijklm
nopqrstuvwxyz
1234567890
(äöü!?&ß$£)

43 pt

Beton
Heinrich Jost, 1931
www.linotype.com

STYMIE

Blitzschutz
isolierfähig
haltbar

50 pt

A B C D E F G H I
J K L M N O P Q R
S T U V W X Y Z
a b c d e f g h i j k l m
n o p q r s t u v w x y z
1 2 3 4 5 6 7 8 9 0
(ä ö ü ! ? & ß $ £)

43 pt

Stymie
Morris Fuller Benton, 1931
www.linotype.com

MAGNUM

MARGARINE

90 pt

ABCDEFGHI
JKLMNOPQR
STUVWXYZ
ABCDEFGHIJKLM
NOPQRSTUVWXYZ
1234567890
(!?&$:;)

45 pt

Magnum
Fontalicious Fonts, 2001
www.fontalicious.com

[illegible] CD

The Black Keys
Poster
Dan Ibarra, Michael Byzewski, 2004

PLAK

Brauerei

95 pt

ABCDEFGHI
JKLMNOPQR
STUVWXYZ
abcdefghijklm
nopqrstuvwxyz
1234567890
(äöü!?&ß$£€@)

40 pt

Plak
Paul Renner, 1930
www.linotype.com

BELL GOTHIC BLACK

Hinterzimmer

70 pt

A B C D E F G H I
J K L M N O P Q R
S T U V W X Y Z
a b c d e f g h i j k l m
n o p q r s t u v w x y z
1 2 3 4 5 6 7 8 9 0
(ä ö ü ! ? & ß $ £)

38 pt

Bell Gothic Black
Chauncey H. Griffith, 1937
www.linotype.com

Herren mit ſtarkem Bartwuchs

schonen ihre Klingen durch Verwendung der „Peri Rasier-Creme" Dieses Radikalmittel bezwingt den stärksten Bart. Reichliche Anwendung von Wasser beim Einpinseln macht das Haar besonders weich; der sahnige Schaum erweicht die Haare bis in die Haarwurzeln. Nur ein Pinsel, kein Rasierbecken, ist erforderlich. Eine Minute Einschäumen mit warmem oder kaltem Wasser genügt, um den Bart schnittreif zu machen. Einreiben mit den Fingern ist überflüssig; denn „Peri Rasier-Creme" schafft's ganz allein. Unnötig ist das Vor- und Nachbehandeln der Haut; denn die Haut wird nicht gereizt. „Peri" spart Zeit und Geld und vermeidet viel Ärger. Darum werden auch Sie Perianer!

Dr. Albersheim's

Peri Rasier-Creme

Peri Rasier-Creme
Advertisement, c. 1930

PILSEN PLAKAT

Durchfchlag

75 pt

A B C D E F G H I
J K L M N O P Q R
S T U V W X Y Z
a b c d e f g h i j k l m
n o p q r s t u v w x y z
1 2 3 4 5 6 7 8 9 0
(ä ö ü ! ? & fi fch f ß $ £)

35 pt

Pilsen Plakat
Dieter Steffmann, 2000
www.steffmann.de

☞ CD

POST-ANTIQUA

Es ist ein Gebot der Klugheit, geistige Nahrung nur aus erster Hand zu nehmen. Der Körperkultur folgt die Pflege der Seele und des Geistes. Man begreift heute, nur dann ist die Gesundung des Lebens möglich.

15 pt

ABCDEFGHI
JKLMNOPQR
STUVWXYZ
abcdefghijklm
nopqrstuvwxyz
1234567890
(äöü!?&fiflß$£)

40 pt

Post-Antiqua
Herbert Post, 1932
www.bertholdtypes.com

ALBERTUS

Zoologischer Garten

65 pt

ABCDEFGHI
JKLMNOPQR
STUVWXYZ
abcdefghijklm
nopqrstuvwxyz
1234567890
(äöü!?&ß$£)

40 pt

Albertus
Berthold Wolpe, 1940
www.linotype.com

FETTE THANNHAEUSER

Für Werbemittel, Verpackungen und Kartonagen wird im neuen Deutschland zäh an ihren alten Aufgaben sowohl zum Wohle des deutschen Graphikers als auch des Fabrikanten von Werbe- und Verpackungsmitteln festgehalten.

15 pt

A B C D E F G H I
J K L M N O P Q R
S T U V W X Y Z
a b c d e f g h i j k l m
n o p q r ſ s t u v w x y z
ä ö ü 1 2 3 4 5 6 7 8 9 0
(! ? & fi fl ſch ch ck ß $ £ †)

38 pt

Fette Thannhaeuser
Dieter Steffmann, 2001
Herbert Thannhaeuser, 1937–38
www.steffmann.de

CD

FETTE TRUMP-DEUTSCH

Eine maleriſche Schrift von Georg Trump,
dem Leiter der Münchner Meiſterſchule, entwickelt
aus der alt-engliſchen Gotiſch zu einem neuen
Eigenleben voller Formenreichtum.

14 pt

A B C D E F G H I
J K L M N O P Q R
S T U V W X Y Z
a b c d e f g h i j k l m
n o p q r ſ s t u v w x y z
ä ö ü 1 2 3 4 5 6 7 8 9 0
! ? & fi fl ff ſch ſſ ſt ch ck ß @

36 pt

Fette Trump-Deutsch
Dieter Steffmann, 2002
Georg Trump, H. Berthold, 1936
www.steffmann.de

CD

DEUTSCH-GOTISCH

Auskunft

90 pt

A A B C D E F G H I
J K L M N O P Q R
S T U V W Y X Z
a b c d e f f g h i j k l m
n o p q r ſ s t u v w x y z
ä ö ü 1 2 3 4 5 6 7 8 9 0
! ? & fi fl ft ſſ ſt tz ch ck

40 pt

Deutsch-Gotisch
Dieter Steffmann, 2002
www.steffmann.de

☞ CD

WERBEDEUTSCH

Nicht alles kann und darf Schema sein!
Eigenart ist das, was uns immer interessiert.
Auch bei der Schrift sagt uns die persönliche
Form mehr, und gerade bei einer deutschen Schrift
wird sie uns immer besser gefallen.

15 pt

A B C D E F G H I
J K L M N O P Q R
S T U V W X Y Z
a b c d e f g h i j k l m
n o p q r ſ s t u v w x y z
ä ö ü 1 2 3 4 5 6 7 8 9 0 ch ck
! ? & ff ſt fl fi ſch ß @

36 pt

Werbedeutsch
Dieter Steffmann, 2002
Herbert Thannhaeuser, 1934
www.steffmann.de

☞ CD

Deutsche Reichspost
Poster
Ludwig Hohlwein, 1935

POTSDAM

Reichspost

90 pt

A B C D E F G H I
J K L M N O P Q R
S T U V W X Y Z
a b c d e f g h i j k l m
n o p q r ſ s t u v w x y z
ä ö ü 1 2 3 4 5 6 7 8 9 0
! ? ﬁ ſt ſſ ck ch tz ß @ : ;

36 pt

Potsdam
Manfred Klein, 2005
Robert Golpon, 1934
www.moorstation.org/typoasis/blackletter

☞ CD

TANNENBERG FETT

Der echte Ausdruck neuer Deutscher

Formgebung

27 / 80 pt

ABCDEFGHI
JKLMNOPQR
STUVWXYZ
abcdefghijklm
nopqrſstuvwxyz
äöü1234567890
! ? & tz ſt ch ck ſſ ſl ff ſch ß

40 pt

Tannenberg Fett
Dieter Steffmann, 2002
Erich Meyer, 1933–35
www.steffmann.de

☞ CD

Campaign against neo-fascist
propaganda on the internet
Poster
Uwe Lösch, 2000

FANFARE

Schlagzeile

85 pt

ABCDEFGHI
JKLMNOPQR
STUVWXYZ
abcdefghijklm
nopqrstuvwxyz
äöü1234567890
(&ß!?$£)

45 pt

Fanfare
Louis Oppenheim, 1927
www.urwpp.com

NEULAND

STEIN
METZ

80 pt

ABCDEFGHI
JKLMNOP
QRSTUVWX
YZÄÖÜ
1234567890
(&!?$£€@)

45 pt

Neuland
Rudolf Koch, 1922
www.linotype.com

STAHL
SKELETT
FÜR DEN GROSSGESCHOSSBAU

VORZÜGE

Festigkeit
Standsicherheit
Raumersparnis
Leichtigkeit
Schnelles Bauen
Methodische
Bauorganisation
Umbaufähigkeit
Haltbarkeit
Feuersicherheit und
Blitzschutz
Isolierfähigkeit
Moderne Bebauungsform
Durchgehende Bauzeit
Hygiene
Wirtschaftlichkeit

Beratungsstelle für Stahlverwendung
DORTMUND·STAHLHOF

Stahlhof Dortmund
Advertisement, 1930

MEMPHIS

Stahlbau

90 pt

ABCDEFGHI
JKLMNOPQR
STUVWXYZ
abcdefghijklm
nopqrstuvwxyz
1234567890
(äöü!?&ß$£)

40 pt

Memphis
Rudolf Wolf, 1930
www.linotype.com

FLAMME

Sonntagsbeilage

85 pt

A B C D E F G H I
J K L M N O P Q R
S T U V W X Y Z
a b c d e f g h i j k l m
n o p q r s t u v w x y z
ä ö ü 1 2 3 4 5 6 7 8 9 0
(& fi fl ß ! ? $ £ €)

50 pt

Flamme
Alan Meeks, 1993
www.linotype.com

MATURA MT

Historische Werke

52 pt

ABCDEFGHI
JKLMNOPQR
STUVWXYZ
abcdefghijklm
nopqrstuvwxyz
äöü1234567890
(&fifl ß!?$£€)

47 pt

Matura MT
Imre Reiner, 1938
www.linotype.com

BLACKHAUS

Omnibus

115 pt

ABCDEFGHI
JKLMNOPQR
STUVWXYZ
abcdefghhijkklm
noppqrrſsttuvwxyz
äöü1234567890
(!?&ffſtß$£@)

38 pt

Blackhaus
Patrick Griffin, 2005
Peterpaul Weiß, 1937
www.canadatype.com

WEISS RUNDGOTISCH

Ja, Sie werden ſogar den Wunſch haben,
auch anderen das eindrucksvolle Werbeſtück zu zeigen,
und damit die Werbewirkung für den Abſender
ungewollt vermehrfachen.

18 pt

A B C D E F G H I
J K L M N O P Q R
S T U V W X Y Z
a b c d e f g h i j k l m
n o p q r ſ s t u v w x y z
ä ö ü 1 2 3 4 5 6 7 8 9 0
(! ? & ß $ £ *)

45 pt

Weiss Rundgotisch
Dieter Steffmann, 1998
Emil Rudolf Weiss, 1937
www.steffmann.de

CD

LEATHER

Gotika

150 pt

ABCDEFGHI
JKLMNOPQR
STUVWXYZ
abcdefghijklm
nopqrsſtuvwxyz
äöü1234567890
!?&ff fi fl ſſ ch ck ß $ £ €

36 pt

Leather
Patrick Griffin, 2005
»Gotika«, Imre Reiner, 1933
www.canadatype.com

Erſtes Deutſches Rapsfett

Das neue
Koch=, Back=, Brat= und Streichfett

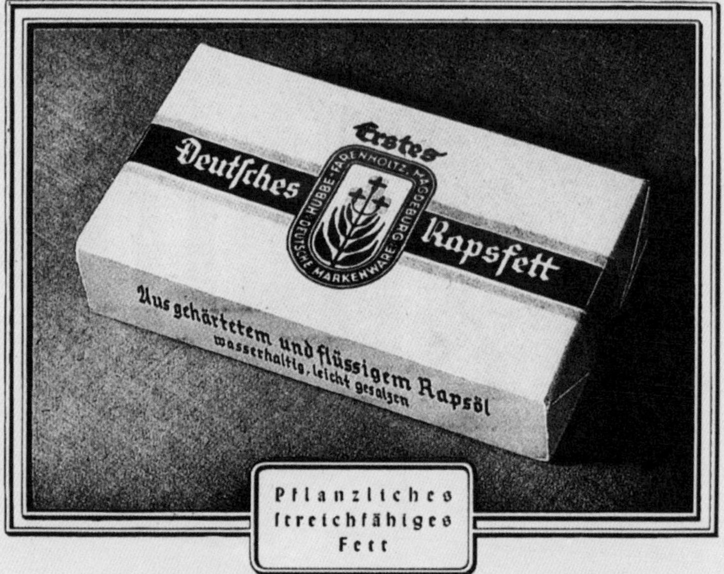

enthält nur einen Fettrohſtoff:
reines deutſches Rapsöl

Vereinigte Ölfabriken Hubbe & Farenholtz
MAGDEBURG

1100

Deutsches Rapsfett
Advertisement, 1940

BRAHMS-GOTISCH

Man ſagt über Johannes Brahms, ſeine Muſik ſei perſönlich und männlich, oft ſchlicht und einfach, dem Volksmäßigen verwandt, dann wieder ungewöhnlich in ihrer Mannigfaltigkeit, immer aber prägnant und feſt geformt. Sind das nicht Worte, die man auch über dieſe ſchöne gotiſche Buchſchrift ſetzen könnte?

16 pt

ABCDEFGHI

JKLMNOPQR

STUVWXYZ

abcdefghijklm

nopqrſstuvwxyz

äöü1234567890

!?&Äßtzffſſftß:;

32 pt

Brahms-Gotisch
Heinz Beck, 1937
www.moorstation.org/typoasis/blackletter

☞ CD

Das Blatt der Hausfrau (later Brigitte)
Magazine cover, 1934

NORDLAND

Ehegatte

145 pt

A B C D E F G H I
J K L M N O P Q R
S T U V W X Y Z
a b c d e f g h i j k l m
n o p q r ſ s t u v w x y z
ä ö ü 1 2 3 4 5 6 7 8 9 0
(! ? & ß ch ck ff tz ph €)

40 pt

Nordland
Petra Heidorn, 2005
Heinz Beck, 1935
www.moorstation.org/typoasis/blackletter

☞ CD

NOUGAT

Bureau

105 pt

ABCDEFGHI
JKLMNOPQR
STUVWXYZ
abcdefghijklm
nopqrstuvwxyz
äöü 1 2 3 4 5 6 7 8 9 0
(&ˇ!?$£*)

42 pt

Nougat
Dieter Steffmann, 2000
www.steffmann.de

☞ CD

LOUISIANNE

Boutique

95 pt

ABCDEFGHI
JKLMNOPQR
STUVWXYZ
abcdefghijklm
nopqrstuvwxyz
äöü1234567890
(„&!?$£§“)

42 pt

Louisianne
Dieter Steffmann, 2000
www.steffmann.de

☞ CD

OKAY

Käsetheke

105 pt

ABCDEFGHI
JKLMNOPQR
STUVWXYZ
abcdefghijklm
nopqrstuvwxyz
äöü1234567890
(»!?&ß£$:;«)

45 pt

Okay
Edwin W. Shaar, 1939
www.linotype.com

FLASH

Angebot

120 pt

ABCDEFGHI
JKLMNOPQR
STUVWXYZ
abcdefghijklm
nopqrstuvwxyz
äöü1234567890
(»!?&ß£$:;«)

45 pt

Flash
Edwin W. Shaar, 1939
www.urwpp.com

TIEMANN

Wenn Sie wüßten, wie roh selbst gebildete Menschen sich gegen die schätzbarsten Kunstwerke verhalten, Sie würden mir verzeihen, wenn ich die meinigen nicht unter die Menge bringen mag.

16 pt

A B C D E F G H I
J K L M N O P Q R
S T U V W X Y Z
a b c d e f g h i j k l m
n o p q r s t u v w x y z
1 2 3 4 5 6 7 8 9 0
ä ö ü ! ? & ﬁ ﬂ ß $ £ € : ;

40 pt

Tiemann
Walter Tiemann, 1923
www.linotype.com

Teppichhaus Repper
Poster and logo
Leslie Cabarga, c. 2000

CANDIDA BOLD

Das Heim ist die erste und wichtigste Schule des Charakters. Hier erhält der Mensch seine beste oder schlechteste Erziehung; denn hier werden all die Grundsätze jenes Benehmens aufgenommen, das uns durch das reifere Alter begleitet und erst mit unserem Leben endigt.

15 pt

A B C D E F G H I
J K L M N O P Q R
S T U V W X Y Z
a b c d e f g h i j k l m
n o p q r s t u v w x y z
1 2 3 4 5 6 7 8 9 0
(ä ö ü ! ? & ß $ £)

41 pt

Candida Bold
Jakob Erbar, 1936
www.linotype.com

RENNER ANTIQUA

Gartenblumen aller Art
Dahlien in 43 Sorten
Rosen, Petunien, Nelken

41 pt

A B C D E F G H I
J K L M N O P Q R
S T U V W X Y Z
a b c d e f g h i j k l m
n o p q r s t u v w x y z
ä ö ü 1 2 3 4 5 6 7 8 9 0
(! ? & ﬁ ﬂ ß $ £ € @ : ;)

41 pt

Renner Antiqua
Patrick Strietzel, 2008
Paul Renner, 1939
www.linotype.com

BERNHARD MODERN

Photography gives concrete form to the subtles thoughts.
It has the gift of imparting to the dullest, most mechanical
and impersonal things the sensitiveness and poetry
which admits them into our dreams.

15 pt

ABCDEFGHI
JKLMNOPQR
STUVWXYZ
abcdefghijklm
nopqrstuvwxyzäöü
1234567890
(„&fiflß!?$£€†")

45 pt

Bernhard Modern
Lucian Bernhard, 1929
www.linotype.com

MONOTYPE BERNARD CONDENSED

New model hosiery. Dresses direct from Paris.

Stylish imported velour hats.

Pottery brass bed piano.

Beautyful chinese rugs linoleum.

15 pt

ABCDEFGHIJKLM

NOPQRSTUVWXYZ

abcdefghijklm

nopqrstuvwxyzäöü

1234567890

(»&ﬁﬂß!?$£€†*«)

40 pt

Monotype Bernard Condensed
Lucian Bernard, 1912
www.linotype.com

EDITION

WETTBUREAU

110 pt

A B C D E F G H I

J K L M N O P Q R

S T U V W X Y Z

1 2 3 4 5 6 7 8 9 0

(! ? & $ @ : ;)

60 pt

Edition
1992
www.dafont.com

☞ CD

ONYX

Olympia

160 pt

A B C D E F G H I J K L M

N O P Q R S T U V W X Y Z

a b c d e f g h i j k l m

n o p q r s t u v w x y z

ä ö ü 1 2 3 4 5 6 7 8 9 0

(» ! ? & ß £ $: ; «)

45 pt

Onyx
Gerry Powell, 1937
www.linotype.com

Delta cigarette factory
Advertisement, 1930

ROCKWELL

Schall und Rauch

65 pt

ABCDEFGHI
JKLMNOPQR
STUVWXYZ
abcdefghijklm
nopqrstuvwxyz
1234567890
(äöü!?&ß$£)

40 pt

Rockwell
Monotype Design Studio, 1934
www.linotype.com

BLOCK BERTHOLD

Ringmeßhaus

85 pt

ABCDEFGHI
JKLMNOPQR
STUVWXYZ
abcdefghijklm
nopqrstuvwxyz
1234567890
(äöü&!?$£*)

40 pt

Block Berthold
H. Hoffmann, 1908–27
www.adobe.com/type

RUNDFUNK GROTESK

Funknetz

85 pt

ABCDEFGHI
JKLMNOPQR
STUVWXYZ
abcdefghijklm
nopqrstuvwxyz
1234567890
(äöü&!?$£€@)

45 pt

Rundfunk Grotesk
Linotype Design Studio, 1933–35
www.linotype.com

SAVINGSBOND

Putzteufel

100 pt

ABCDEFGHI
JKLMNOPQR
STUVWXYZ
abcdefghijklm
nopqrstuvwxyz
äöü1234567890
!?&ß£$€:;

42 pt

SavingsBond
Harold Lohner, 1998
www.haroldsfonts.com

☞ CD

Clean & Co. LLC
Packaging
Sharon Werner, Sarah Nelson c. 2000

Diatype phototypesetting machine, manufactured between 1952 and 1960

Petticoats and Rock'n'Roll Organic Design and Calligraphic Style

c. 1945–1960

At the end of World War II Germany was in ruins. In the context of countless casualties, prisoners-of-war, tales of escape and subsequent expulsion, acute homelessness, hunger and cold no one was concerned with typography. As designers began to get their bearings again, the domination of two typefaces – New Gothic and Antique – finally came to an end. The occupying forces could not read the fractured scripts anyway, and no one wanted to be misinterpreted as standing in the way of de-Nazification. Moreover, there was a desire to comply with international standards, standards to which roman letters were better suited.

Vier Perlen
Poster, 1952

Petticoats and Rock'n'Roll Organic Design and Calligraphic Style

c. 1945–1960

GypsyRose
2000 | page 334

Looking back, poster and brushed scripts seemed to be ubiquitous. But type designs of this kind were not novelties of the fifties. Much earlier, the advertising industry used fonts that simulated the liveliness of a brushstroke. However, in the post-war period, they became all the rage, and thus a variety of new styles were created. In addition, more and more typefaces looked as though they were written with a quill pen.

Classical Antique in its more extreme styles – extra-narrow, extra-thick, extra-wide – also enjoyed a renaissance. Less so the classic, severe typefaces – though they were permitted a certain playfulness that sometimes resulted in an original design. In some cases space was filled with floral motifs. Other designs highly compressed the letters or gave them a new interpretation through the modification of their fundamental forms. The extreme contrast between hairline and broad strokes might be said to match the tastes of this period, if one looks to compare trends in furniture design (kidney shapes with exceedingly thin legs) and art.

Scripts with accentuated serifs, sometimes shaded or enhanced, also enjoyed a certain popularity. They put a typographical face on American rock 'n' roll and jazz, for example. Newspapers use their striking appearance for title pages, and various logos and advertisements appeared on the scene with self-consciously accentuated serifs.

Typefaces

Classical Antiqua

Characteristics

Reporter

These scripts simulate spontaneous, lively brush-strokes. Their dynamic and robust form is highly characteristic of post-war typography.

Poster and brushed scripts

Characteristics

In their general character, these type designs remain very close to the traditional handwritten styles of the preceding century. They give the appearance of having been written with a quill pen.

Calligraphic scripts

Characteristics

Airstream

These handwritten scripts, which have an experimental appearance, are the typographical equivalent to 'streamlined' design. Their unique character comes from the contact between letters along the baseline.

Handwritten scripts with an experimental character

Characteristics

Trump Gothic

In the fifties, a specific type of Grotesque script became highly sought after, distinguished by narrow letters and counters and a high x-height.

Narrow sans-serif scripts

Characteristics

Schadow

Variants of Antique during this time were modelled on scripts with accentuated serifs as well as classical or calligraphic scripts, though they are often more playful and decorative than the original models.

Variants of Antiqua

Characteristics

SAPHIR

In the existing repertoire of classical typefaces there emerged a preference for narrow and thick styles. New designs of the period were altogether more playful and less severe than the originals.

Characteristics

Example:
Saphir
Hermann Zapf
1950 | page 335

Example:
Schadow Black
Georg Trump
1952 | page 318

Example:
Trump Gothic (East)
Georg Trump
1955 | page 340

Example:
Airstream
Nick Curtis
2000 | page 322

Example:
Diskus
Martin Wilke
1938 | page 299

Example:
Reporter #2
Carlos Winkow
1938 | page 311

Typefaces

In body text, fractured scripts became obsolete, and only Antique – and, occasionally, Grotesque – came into play.

In addition to poster and brushed scripts, handwritten and calligraphic scripts were popular for record covers, posters, ads and logos. Classical Antique enjoyed a comeback, not in its traditional role as body text, but rather as a display type. Type designs with accentuated serifs and in lighter styles were also popular.

Text and illustration

Lines in the popular brushed scripts were set diagonally in order to reinforce their spontaneous character. Monochrome black-and-white illustrations with harsh lighting were in fashion. In addition, books were illustrated – often by hand – with linocuts or simple colour fields.

Ornaments

Organic forms (especially kidney shapes) together with thin lines, were often employed as decorative devices.

Die Sünderin
Poster, c. 1950

DISKUS

Hildegard

105 pt

A B C D E F G H I
J K L M N O P Q R
S T U V W X Y Z

a b c d e f g h i j k l m

n o p q r s t u v w x y z ä ö ü

1 2 3 4 5 6 7 8 9 0

(! ? ﬂ ﬁ & ß £ $)

38 pt

Diskus
Martin Wilke, 1938
www.linotype.com

BOULEVARD

Smaragd

90 pt

A B C D E F G H I

J K L M N O P Q R

S T U V W X Y Z

a b c d e f g h i j k l m

n o p q r s t u v w x y z

ä ö ü 1 2 3 4 5 6 7 8 9 0

(» ! ? fi fl & ß £ $ «)

32 pt

Boulevard
Günter Gerhard Lange, 1955
www.bertholdtypes.com

CHARME

Tütenlampe

95 pt

ABCDEFGHI
JKLMNOPQR
STUVWXYZ
abcdefghijklm
nopqrstuvwxyz
äöü1234567890
(!?fiflߣ$:;)

42 pt

Charme
Helmut Matheis, 1957
www.linotype.com

MISTRAL

Urlaubsfieber

90 pt

ABCDEFGHI
JKLMNOPQR
STUVWXYZ
abcdefghijklm
nopqrstuvwxyz
äöü1234567890
(»fifl!?&ß£$€«)

45 pt

Mistral
Roger Excoffon, 1953
www.linotype.com

CHAMPION

Buchauslage

95 pt

A B C D E F G H I
J K L M N O P Q R
S T U V W X Y Z
a b c d e f g h i j k l m
n o p q r s t u v w x y z
ä ö ü 1 2 3 4 5 6 7 8 9 0
» ! ? & ß $ £ «

42 pt

Champion
Günter Gerhard Lange, 1957
www.bertholdtypes.com

BULLPEN 3D

Bärenstark

60 pt

A B C D E F G H I
J K L M N O P Q R
S T U V W X Y Z
a b c d e f g h i j k l m
n o p q r s t u v w x y z
ä ö ü 1 2 3 4 5 6 7 8 9 0
! ? & ß £ $ € @ : ;

35 pt

Bullpen 3D
Ray Larabie, 2001
www.larabiefonts.com

☞ CD

'Berlin – Seen by AGI'
Exhibition catalogue
Fons Hickmann m23, 2005

HOLLA

Strumpfhose

100 pt

A B C D E F G H I
J K L M N O P Q R
S T U V W X Y Z
a b c d e f g h i j k l m
n o p q r s t u v w x y z
ä ö ü 1 2 3 4 5 6 7 8 9 0
(! ? ch ck & ß £ $)

45 pt

Holla
Dieter Steffmann, 2001
www.steffmann.de

☞ CD

TEAMSPIRIT

Football

100 pt

A B C D E F G H I

J K L M N O P Q R

S T U V W X Y Z

a b c d e f g h i j k l m

n o p q r s t u v w x y z

1 2 3 4 5 6 7 8 9 0

ä ö ü & ß st nd rd th

40 pt

TeamSpirit
Nick Curtis, 2000
www.dafont.com

CD

Vespa
Advertisement, 1956

QUIGLEY WIGGLY

Motorroller

100 pt

A B C D E F G H I
J K L M N O P Q R
S T U V W X Y Z
a b c d e f g h i j k l m
n o p q r s t u v w x y z
ä ö ü 1 2 3 4 5 6 7 8 9 0
(! ? & ß £ $ €)

45 pt

Quigley Wiggly
Nick Curtis, 2000
www.dafont.com

☞ CD

CHOC

Schlager

130 pt

ABCDEFGHI
JKLMNOPQR
STUVWXYZ
abcdefghijklm
nopqrstuvwxyz
äöü1234567890
(!?fiffl&ß£$:;)

47 pt

Choc
Roger Excoffon, 1955
www.linotype.com

REPORTER #2

Extrablatt

110 pt

ABCDEFGHI
JKLMNOPQR
STUVWXYZ
abcdefghijklm
nopqrstuvwxyz
äöü1234567890
(!?fiffl&ßE£$:;)

42 pt

Reporter #2
Carlos Winkow, 1938
www.linotype.com

MERCURIUS SCRIPT

Grobkörnig

75 pt

A B C D E F G H I
J K L M N O P Q R
S T U V W X Y Z
a b c d e f g h i j k l m
n o p q r s t u v w x y z
ä ö ü 1 2 3 4 5 6 7 8 9 0
» ! ? ﬁ ﬂ & ß $ £ «

42 pt

Mercurius Script
Imre Reiner, 1957
www.linotype.com

Astaire + Riefenstahl
Poster
Mende Design, 2007

MELIOR

Madame begeistert die große Welt.
Sie ist klug und charmant,
ihr Geschmack ist unbestechlich.

20 pt

ABCDEFGHI
JKLMNOPQR
STUVWXYZ
abcdefghijklm
nopqrstuvwxyz
äöü1234567890
(»!?&ß£$:;«)

42 pt

Melior
Hermann Zapf, 1952
www.linotype.com

SISTINA

URKUNDE

87 pt

ABCDEFGHI
JKLMNOPQR
STUVWXYZ
ABCDEFGHIJKLM
NOPQRSTUVWXYZ
ÄÖÜ1234567890
(»!?&£$€@:;«)

42 pt

Sistina
Hermann Zapf, 1950
www.linotype.com

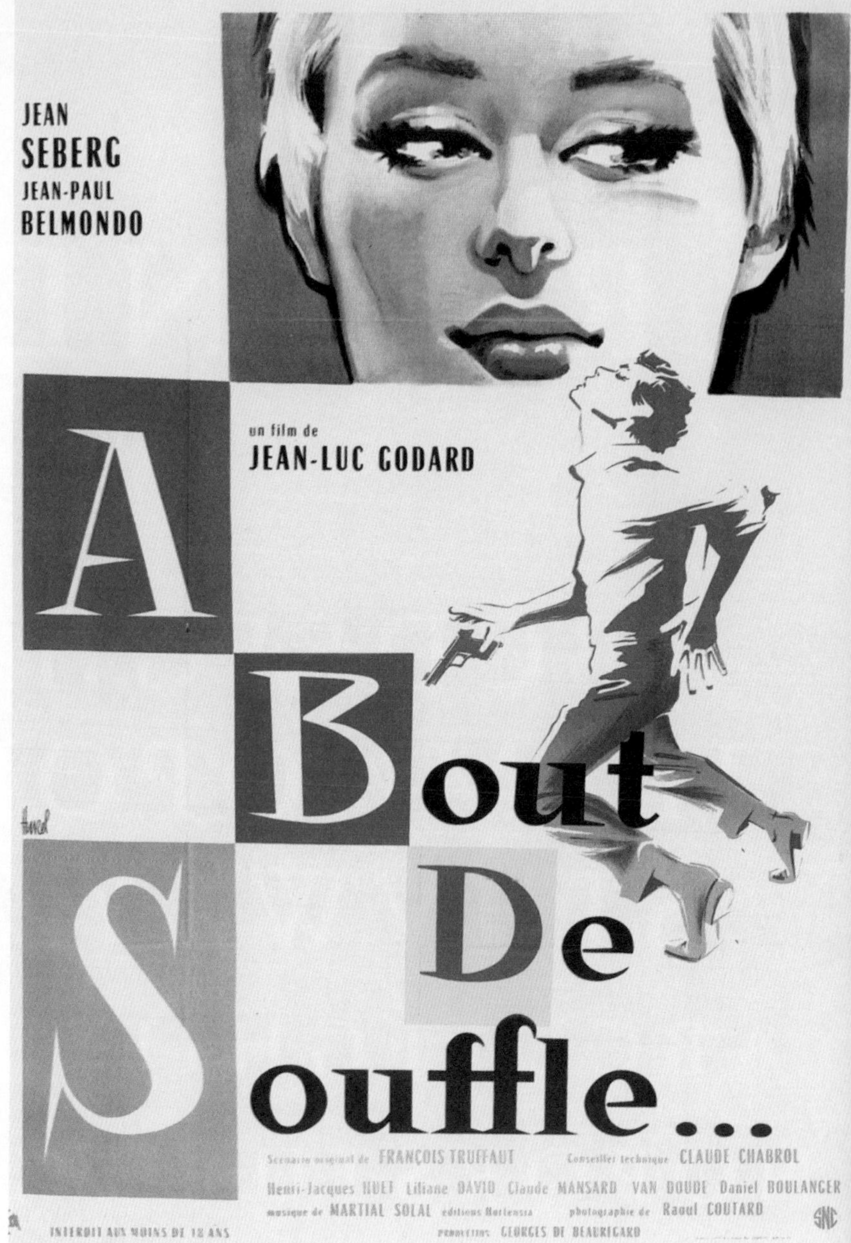

A Bout De Souffle
Poster, 1959

PIKE

All about Love

115 / 91 pt

A B C D E F G H I
J K L M N O P Q R
S T U V W X Y Z
a b c d e f g h i j k l m
n o p q r s t u v w x y z
ä ö ü 1 2 3 4 5 6 7 8 9 0
(» ! ? & ß £ $ «)

45 pt

Pike
Panache Graphics, 1992
www.fonthaus.com

SCHADOW BLACK

Ihre Briefe sind schon optisch aus der Fülle täglich eingehender Post hervorgehoben, wenn sie mit farbiger Tesaborde eingefasst sind. Durch die suggestive Kraft der Farbe wird immer zuerst nach diesen Briefen gegriffen.

20 pt

A B C D E F G H I
J K L M N O P Q R
S T U V W X Y Z
a b c d e f g h i j k l m
n o p q r s t u v w x y z
ä ö ü 1 2 3 4 5 6 7 8 9 0
(» ! ? & ß £ $: ; «)

40 pt

Schadow Black
Georg Trump, 1952
www.bitstream.com

FORUM I

REKORD

90 pt

A B C D E F G
H I J K L M N O
P Q R S T U V
W X Y Z Ä Ö Ü
1 2 3 4 5 6 7 8 9 0
(» ! ? & £ $: ; «)

45 pt

Forum I
Georg Trump, 1952
www.myfonts.com

GRENOUILLE

Handlesen

145 pt

ABCDEFGHI
JKLMNOPQR
STUVWXYZ
abcdeffghijklm
nnopqrstuvwxyz
äöü1234567890
!?fififfffiffl&&€@

42 pt

Grenouille
Louis Rigaud
www.dafont.com

☞ CD

Extremely Loud & Incredibly Close
Book cover
Jon Gray, 2004

AIRSTREAM

The Airport

100 pt

ABCDEFGHI
JKLMNOPQR
STUVWXYZ
abcdefghijklm
nopqrstuvwxyz
äöü/1234567890
»!?&ß£$€ the «

48 pt

Airstream
Nick Curtis, 2000
www.dafont.com

CD

KAUFMANN

Tanzschule

90 pt

ABCDEFGHI
JKLMNOPQR
STUVWXYZ
abcdefghijklm
nopqrstuvwxyz
äöü1234567890
(!?fiffl&ß£$:;)

42 pt

Kaufmann
Max R. Kaufmann, 1936
www.linotype.com

Mon Oncle

PRÄDIKAT WERTVOLL

EIN FILM VON
JACQUES TATI

d'après P. ÉTAIX

Drehbuch und Dialoge nach einer Idee von JACQUES TATI
in künstlerischer Zusammenarbeit mit JACQUES LEGRANG
und JEAN L'HOTE
Produktion: SPECTA FILMS/GRAY FILM/ALTER FILMS
Verleih

GILLIES GOTHIC

Kinocafé

150 pt

ABCDEFGHI
JKLMNOPQR
STUVWXYZ
abcdefghijklm
nopqrstuvwxyzäöü
1234567890
(»!?&ß£$@«)

43 pt

Gillies Gothic
William S. Gillies, 1935
www.linotype.com

AIR CONDITIONER

Milchshake

45 pt

ABCDEFGHI

JKLMNOPQR

STUVWXYZ

abcdefghijklm

nopqrstuvwxyz

äöü1234567890

(» ! ? & ß £ $ € : ; «)

29 pt

Air Conditioner
Font Diner, 2002
www.fontdiner.com

☞ CD

DYMAXION SCRIPT

Cabriolet

75 pt

A B C D E F G H I
J K L M N O P Q R
S T U V W X Y Z
a b c d e f g h i j k l m
n o p q r s t u v w x y z
ä ö ü 1 2 3 4 5 6 7 8 9 0
(! ? & ß £ $ € : ;)

42 pt

Dymaxion Script
Nick Curtis, 1999
www.dafont.com

CD

HOOD ORNAMENT

Car wash

90 pt

A B C D E F G H I

J K L M N O P Q R

S T U V W X Y Z

a b c d e f g h i j k l m

n o p q r s t u v w x y z

ä ö ü 1 2 3 4 5 6 7 8 9 0

! ? tt § & ß £ @ «

25 pt

Hood Ornament
2000
www.dafont.com

CD

Splendid
Garage

Splendid Garage
Book cover
Lizá Ramalho, Artur Rebelo, 2008

FUTURA SCRIPT EF

Gummibaum

74 pt

ABCDEFGHI
JKLMNOPQR
STUVWXYZ
abcdefghijklm
nopqrstuvwxyz
äöü1234567890
(»!?&ß£$€@«)

44 pt

Futura Script EF
Paul Renner, 1954
www.fonts4ever.com

ROCKET SCRIPT

Coupé

80 pt

ABCDEFGHI

JKLMNOPQR

STUVWXYZ

abcdefghijklm

nopqrstuvwxyz

äöü1234567890

(» ! ? & ß £ $ @ «)

32 pt

Rocket Script
Font Diner, 2002
www.fontdiner.com

CD

'Ein großer Augenblick!'
Advertisement, 1950

'Froh in den Hausputz'
Advertisement, 1957

ANNLIE

Frühjahr

90 pt

ABCDEFGHI
JKLMNOPQR
STUVWXYZ
abcdefghijklm
nopqrstuvwxyz
1234567890
(»äöü!?&$€@«)

43 pt

Annlie
Fred Lambert, 1966
www.linotype.com

GYPSYROSE

ROSE

100 pt

A A B C D
E F G H I J K
L M N O P
Q R R S T U V
W X Y Z
! ? & : ;

40 pt

GypsyRose
2000
www.dafont.com

☞ CD

SAPHIR

GUTE STUBE

80 pt

ABCDEFG
HIJKLMNO
PQRSTUV
WXYZÄÖÜ
1234567890
!?&$£€@:;

45 pt

Saphir
Hermann Zapf, 1950
www.linotype.com

'Milch in Papier'
Tetrapak advertisement, 1954

CORVINUS

Calcium

135 pt

ABCDEFGHIJKLM
NOPQRSTUVWXYZ
abcdefghijklm
nopqrstuvwxyz
äöü1234567890
(”!?&£$“)

45 pt

Corvinus
Imre Reiner, 1934
www.fonthaus.com

DOLPHIAN

EINLADUNG

50 pt

ABCDEFGHI

JKLMNOPQR

STUVWXYZ

1234567890

»ÄÖÜ!?&£$@«

43 pt

Dolphian
1993
www.dafont.com

☞ CD

SMARAGD

DIPLOM

70 pt

A B C D E F G H I

J K L M N O P Q R

S T U V W X Y Z

1 2 3 4 5 6 7 8 9 0

» Ä Ö Ü ! ? & £ $ «

40 pt

Smaragd
Gudrun Zapf-von Hesse, 1953
www.linotype.com

TRUMP GOTHIC (EAST)

Obstsalat

150 pt

ABCDEFGHIJKLM
NOPQRSTUVWXYZ
abcdefghijklm
nopqrstuvwxyz
äöü1234567890
(»!?&ffiffl£$€@«)

45 pt

Trump Gothic (East)
Georg Trump, 1955
www.canadatype.com

Strawberry Fields
Book cover
Jon Gray, 2004

FUTURA DISPLAY

Nierentisch

100 pt

ABCDEFGHI
JKLMNOPQR
STUVWXYZ
abcdefghijklm
nopqrstuvwxyz
1234567890
(»äöü!?&$€@«)

43 pt

Futura Display
Paul Renner, 1932
www.linotype.com

VICTOR

Milchmann

100 pt

A B C D E F G H I
J K L M N O P Q R
S T U V W X Y Z
a b c d e f g h i j k l m
n o p q r s t u v w x y z
1 2 3 4 5 6 7 8 9 0
(» ä ö ü ! ? & : ; * «)

45 pt

Victor
Mare, 2006
www.dafont.com

CD

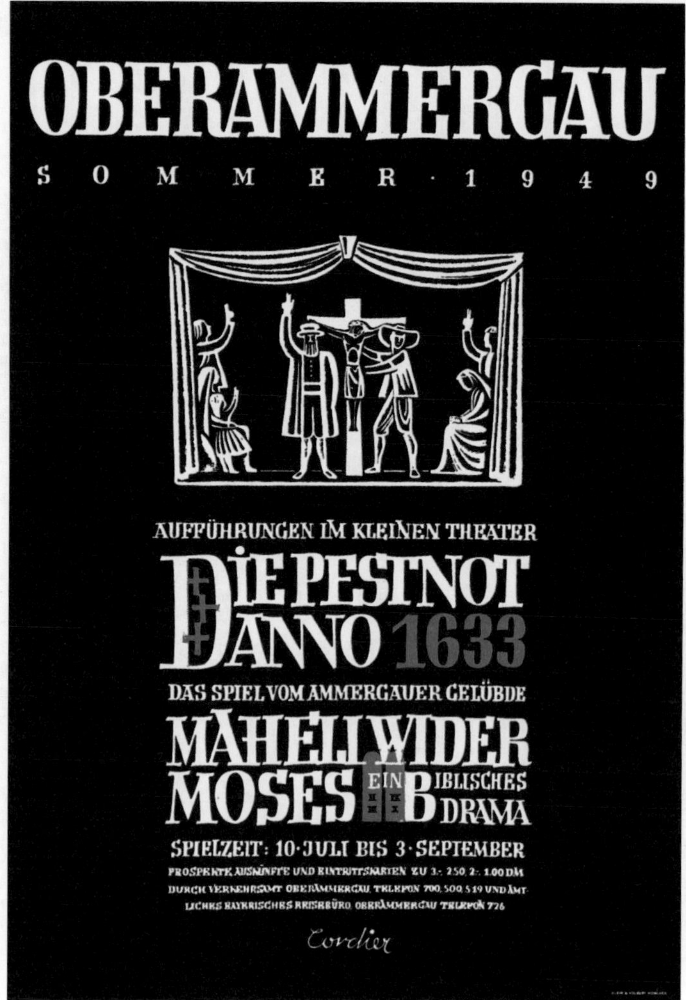

Die Pestnot anno 1633
Poster
Eugen Max Cordier, 1949

DELPHIN

Theater

130 pt

ABCDEFGHI
JKLMNOPQR
STUVWXYZ
abcddefgghijklm
nopqrsstuvwxyz
1234567890
(äöü!?fifl&ß€@)

50 pt

Delphin
Georg Trump, 1952
www.linotype.com

FORELLE

Virtuose

130 pt

A B C D E F G H I
J K L M N O P Q R
S T U V W X Y Z
a b c d e f g h i j k l m
n o p q r s t u v w x y z
ä ö ü 1 2 3 4 5 6 7 8 9 0
(! ? & ß £ $: ;)

45 pt

Forelle
Dieter Steffmann, 2000
www.steffmann.de

CD

MARCELLE SCRIPT & SWASHES

100 pt

ABCDEFGHI
JKLMNOPQR
STUVWXYZ
abcdefghijklm
nopqrstuvwxyz
1234567890
(!?&*:;)

45 pt

Marcelle Script & Swashes
StereoType, 2003
www.stereo-type.net

CD

BRUSH SCRIPT

Ausgehfein

90 pt

ABCDEFGHI
JKLMNOPQR
STUVWXYZ
abcdefff ghijklm
nopp qrstuvwxyz
1234567890
äöü!?fifl&ß$£

40 pt

Brush Script
Robert E. Smith, 1953
www.linotype.com

Cha Cha Haircut Lounge,
Brochure
Planet Propaganda, 2000

EXPRESS

Fangfrisch

100 pt

ABCDEFGHI
JKLMNOPQR
STUVWXYZ
abcdefghijklm
nopqrstuvwxyz
äöü1234567890
(»!?&ß£$:;«)

40 pt

Express
Dieter Steffmann, 1999
www.steffmann.de

CD

SALTO

Hula Hoop

120 pt

A B C D E F G H I
J K L M N O P Q R
S T U V W X Y Z
a b c d e f g h i j k l m
n o p q r s t u v w x y z
ä ö ü 1 2 3 4 5 6 7 8 9 0
(! ? & fi fl ß £ $ € @)

48 pt

Salto
Karlgeorg Hoefer, 1952
www.linotype.com

Das Mädchen Rosemarie
Poster, 1957

Natürlich die Autofahrer
Poster, 1959

ALISON

Adrett

90 pt

A A B C D E F G G H I

J K L M N O P Q R

S T U V W X Y Z

a b c c d e e f g h h i j k k

l m m n n o o p q r r

s s s t t u v w x y z

1 2 3 4 5 6 7 8 9 0 ! ? & @ ✓

30 pt

Alison
Nancy Wall, Robert Wall, 1992
www.dafont.com

☞ CD

wirt wun
schafts der

Helvetica
Max Miedinger
1957 | page 392

1955
—
1968

Heidelberg letterpress, manufactured in the 1960s

space age

Amelia
Stanley Davis
1965 | page 374

W

Economic Miracle and Moon Landing Swiss Typography and the Space Age

c. 1955–1968

In Switzerland, the idea of Elementary Typography caught on and was put into everyday practice internationally. Sans-serif typefaces, serial design and rectilinear principles appeared best suited for international communication. The result was a boom in commercial Grotesque followed by a profusion of new styles.

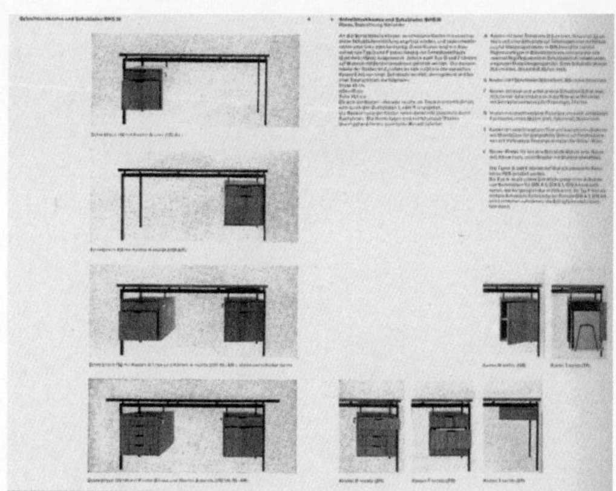

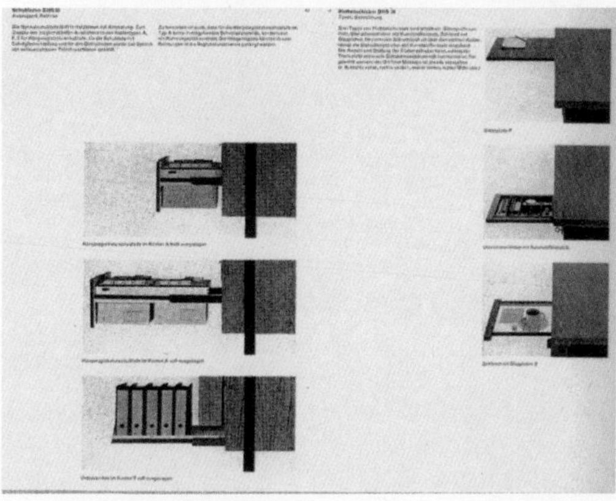

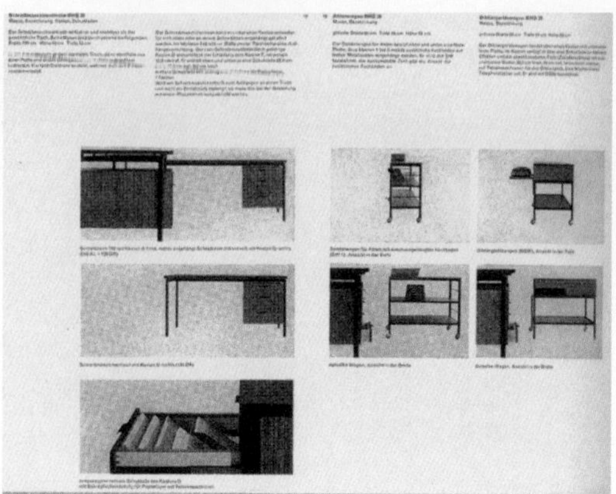

Holzaepfel
Catalogue
Karl Gerstner, c. 1960

Economic Miracle and Moon Landing
Swiss Typography and the Space Age

c. 1955–1968

schweizer typo

Univers
Adrian Frutiger
1954 | page 365

The Hochschule für Gestaltung (HfG) [School of Design] was founded in Ulm in 1953. Here the ideals of the Bauhaus were carried even further with a curriculum based largely on Bauhaus principles. Initially, typography played a minor role in Ulm – the main concerns were architecture and industrial design. The school's unique concern for the theoretical dimension of graphic design and the pioneering study of the semiotics of good design had a significant impact internationally, and this had an eventual effect on typography as well. The concept of corporate design was very new and at Ulm they believed that a company must be readily identifiable in all of its elements.

Because of the high demand for Grotesque scripts that arose out of 'Swiss typography' and the 'Ulm School,' type design houses began to worry about maintaining an adequate supply. The most famous typefaces to emerge at this time were Univers and Helvetica.

Furthermore, technological sensations were making headlines. In 1961, Russian cosmonaut Yuri Gagarin became the first person to orbit the Earth, which started the 'space race' between the Soviet Union and the United States. Such news events influenced type design as well. Accordingly, in the sixties several typefaces were designed that left a technological and modern impression.

Typefaces

Machine-readable fonts

Helvetica

Characteristics

Despite their plain, neutral character, these scripts are drawn rather than artificially constructed. The stroke widths are not uniform and so support better legibility.

Sans-serif scripts with a classical character

Eurostile

Characteristics

Some of the more fashionable scripts of the sixties sprang from the excitement and possibilities resulting from modern technology. Their basic forms appear to have been constructed with the use of technology, and in one case they were inspired by cathode ray tubes.

Technological sans-serif variants of Antiqua

Countdown

Characteristics

During this period, an array of display fonts was developed by designers who were themselves inspired by space travel. The fonts are distinguished by technological transitions and variations in line width.

Space age display fonts

OCR-A

Characteristics

A demand for machine-readable fonts emerged in the sixties. As a result all the letters in an alphabet must be starkly differentiated so that they can be scanned.

Characteristics

Example:
Helvetica
Max Miedinger
1957 | page 392

Example:
Eurostile
Aldo Novarese
1962 | page 404

Example:
Countdown
Colin Brignall
1965 | page 382

Example:
OCR-A
Adrian Frutiger
1968 | page 403

Typefaces

Without exception, sans-serif forms of typefaces were used in objective, functional typography. Besides the types already available, such as commercial Grotesque and Futura, many new Grotesque scripts were brought onto the market. In addition, many new alphabets inspired by the 'space age' became fashionable for use as display scripts.

Text

'Swiss typography' relied exclusively on asymmetrical text, implemented with the fewest possible type styles and sizes. Thus, ample white space had to be effectively integrated with the text. Strict rectilinear principles gave the designs its distinctive character.

Ornaments

Apart from lines and bars there was no embellishment. Photography was separated from explanatory text. Otherwise, plain colours and forms were used in design.

National Zeitung
Corporate design
Karl Gerstner, c. 1960

AKZIDENZ GROTESK

I only accept functional typefaces. The one you are reading right now is the one I preferred for 60 years now. It is **Akzidenz Grotesk**.

Anton Stankowski

25 / 15 pt

A B C D E F G H I
J K L M N O P Q R
S T U V W X Y Z
a b c d e f g h i j k l m
n o p q r s t u v w x y z
1 2 3 4 5 6 7 8 9 0
(ä ö ü ! ? & ß £ $ @ : ;)

40 pt

Akzidenz Grotesk
Günter Gerhard Lange, 1963-68
After a typeface by H. Berthold, 1896
www.bertholdtypes.com

MIEDINGER

SPORT

65 pt

ABCDEFG
HIJKLMNO
PQRSTUV
WXYZÄÖÜ
1234567890
(»!?&@$€:;«)

37 pt

Miedinger
Max Miedinger, Patrick Griffin, 2007
www.canadatype.com

HURTMOLD

Bildröhre

90 pt

ABCDEFGHI
JKLMNOPQR
STUVWXYZ
abcdefghijklm
nopqrstuvwxyz
1234567890
(äöü!?$:;)

49 pt

Hurtmold
Billy Argel, 2007
www.dafont.com

CD

UniversUniversUniversUniversUniversUniversUniversUnivers

Univers – gut lesbar, weil optisch richtig –
eine vernünftige, klare Groteskschrift,
die Logik im Aufbau und ihre Dynamik im Bild
offenbaren sich im Schema der einundzwanzig
sorgfältig aufeinander abgestimmten Schnitte

Setzmaschinen-Fabrik Monotype Gesellschaft m.b.H.
Frankfurt am Main und Berlin
Telefon (0611) 48744 und (0311) 6872485

Monotype eingetragenes Warenzeichen

Univers Création DP

Univers
Advertisement
Monotype GmbH, 1966

UNIVERS

Univers – gut lesbar, weil optisch richtig – eine vernünftige, klare Groteskschrift, die Logik im Aufbau und ihre Dynamik im Bild offenbaren sich im Schema der einundzwanzig sorgfältig aufeinander abgestimmten Schnitte.

16 pt

A B C D E F G H I
J K L M N O P Q R
S T U V W X Y Z
a b c d e f g h i j k l m
n o p q r s t u v w x y z
ä ö ü 1 2 3 4 5 6 7 8 9 0
(» ! ? & ß $ £ @ : ; «)

40 pt

Univers
Adrian Frutiger, 1954
www.linotype.com

STEELFISH

Geheimagent

120 pt

A B C D E F G H I J K L M
N O P Q R S T U V W X Y Z
a b c d e f g h i j k l m
n o p q r s t u v w x y z
1 2 3 4 5 6 7 8 9 0
(! ? & ﬁ ﬂ ß $ € @ : ;)

55 pt

Steelfish
Ray Larabie, 2001
www.larabiefonts.com

CD

MICROGRAMMA LT BOLD EXTENDED

Octopussy
and the Living Daylights

60 / 25 pt

ABCDEFGHI
JKLMNOPQR
STUVWXYZ
abcdefghijklm
nopqrstuvwxyz
1234567890
(!?&fiflß$€@:;)

36 pt

Microgramma LT Bold Extended
A. Butti, Aldo Novarese, 1951
www.linotype.com

Roth-Händle
Poster
Michael Engelmann, 1960

COMPACTA

Raucherbein

120 pt

A B C D E F G H I J K L M
N O P Q R S T U V W X Y Z
a b c d e f g h i j k l m
n o p q r s t u v w x y z
ä ö ü 1 2 3 4 5 6 7 8 9 0
(„ ! ? & ß £ $: ; * ")

50 pt

Compacta
Fred Lambert, 1963
www.linotype.com

ATOMIC

Rotation

150 pt

A B C D E F G H I J K L M

N O P Q R S T U V W X Y Z

a b c d e f g h i j k l m

n o p q r s t u v w x y z

1 2 3 4 5 6 7 8 9 0

(ä ö ü ! ? $: ;)

55 pt

Atomic
Fontalicious Fonts, 1999
www.fontalicious.com

CD

JADE MONKEY

Elektron

100 pt

ABCDEFGHIJKLM
NOPQRSTUVWXYZ
abcdefghijklm
nopqrstuvwxyz
1234567890
äö!?&$

48 pt

Jade Monkey
Claes Kallarsson, 1997–98
www.fuelfonts.com

IMPACT

Mr. President

70 pt

A B C D E F G H I J K L M
N O P Q R S T U V W X Y Z
a b c d e f g h i j k l m
n o p q r s t u v w x y z
1 2 3 4 5 6 7 8 9 0
(ä ö ü ! ? & ß $ £ @ : ;)

42 pt

Impact
Geoffrey Lee, 1965
www.linotype.com

when
it()
reigns,
it()
poors

U.S. President George W. Bush states objective of Iraq invasion:

"To disarm Iraq of weapons of mass destruction, to end Saddam Hussein's support for terrorism, and to free the Iraqi people."

Risk of death in Iraq estimated to be 2.5-fold higher after the invasion.

Risk of death from violence in Iraq estimated to be 58 times higher than the preinvasion period.

1.6 million Iraqi people displaced internally.

1.8 million Iraqi people displaced to neighboring countries.

Estimated 70% of children suffering from trauma-related symptoms.

One fifth of the Iraqi population below the poverty line.

Nearly 400,000 Iraqi children suffer from acute malnutrition.

National Design Centre Melbourne

AMELIA

Sphäre

115 pt

ABCDEFGHIJKLM

NOPQRSTUVWXYZ

abcdefghijklm

nopqrstuvwxyz

äöü1234567890

„!?ﬁﬂ&$:;"

45 pt

Amelia
Stanley Davis, 1965
www.linotype.com

GRAVITY SUCKS

Masse

115 pt

ABCDEFGHI
JKLMNOPQR
STUVWXYZ
abcdefghijklm
nopqrstuvwxyz
1234567890
(äöü!?$@)

43 pt

Gravity Sucks
Rich Gast, 1999
greywolfwebworks.home.insightbb.com

☞ CD

ORBIT-B

Orbiter

115 pt

ABCDEFGHIJKLM

NOPQRSTUVWXYZ

abcdefghijklm

nopqrstuvwxyz

1234567890

(äöü!?&fiflß$)

35 pt

Orbit-B
S. Biggenden, 1972
www.bitstream.com

SPACESHIP BULLET

Spionage

115 pt

A B C D E F G H I J K L M

N O P Q R S T U V W X Y Z

a b c d e f g h i j k l m

n o p q r s t u v w x y z

1 2 3 4 5 6 7 8 9 0

(ä ö ü ! ? & ß $ € @)

47 pt

Spaceship Bullet
Steve Ferrera, 2008
www.dafont.com

CD

Advertising in Italy
Book cover
Franco Grignani, 1972

DATA 70

Advertisement

80 pt

ABCDEFGHI
JKLMNOPQR
STUVWXYZ
abcdefghijklm
nopqrstuvwxyz
1234567890
[äöü!?ﬁﬂ&ß£$]

43 pt

Data 70
Bob Newman, 1970
www.linotype.com

COMPUTERFONT

Personal Computer

60 / 80 pt

ABCDEFGHIJKLM
NOPQRSTUVWXYZ
abcdefghijklm
nopqrstuvwxyz
1234567890
äöü!?&ß@$

45 pt

Computerfont
1992
www.dafont.com

t ☆ CD

DROID LOVER

ANDROID

90 pt

ABCDEF
GHIJKLM
NOPQRS
TUVWXYZ
1234567890
(!?&@$€)

50 pt

Droid Lover
Iconian Fonts, 2008
www.iconian.com

CD

COUNTDOWN

Roboter

140 pt

ABCDEFGHI
JKLMNOPQR
STUVWXYZ
abcdefghijklm
nopqrstuvwxyz
äöü1234567890
(»!?&ß$€:;«)

43 pt

Countdown
Colin Brignall, 1965
www.linotype.com

Tenth Anniversary Tour
Poster
Ames Design, 2001

CHEEK2CHEEK (BLACK!)

TECHNIK

52 pt

A B C D E F G
H I J K L M
N O P Q R S T
U V W X Y Z
1 2 3 4 5 6 7
8 9 0
(! ? = ; *)

30 pt

cheek2cheek (black!)
shk.dezign, 1999
welcome.to/shylock

CD

CHINTZY CPU BRK

SPUTNIK

100 pt

ABCDEFGHI
JKLMNOPQR
STUVWXYZ
ABCDEFGHIJKLM
NOPQRSTUVWXYZ
1234567890
(!?:;*)

43 pt

Chintzy CPU BRK
Ænigma Fonts, 2002
www.acnigmafonts.com

[illegible] CD

apollo

155 pt

a b c d e f g h i

j k l m n o p q r

s t u v w x y z

1 2 3 4 5 6 7 8 9 0

ä ö ü ! ? & $ №

55 pt

PHuture
Jeff Bensch, 2008
jbensch.deviantart.com

[illegible] CD

SPEEDFREEK

midtown

144 pt

A B C D E F G H I J K L M

N O P Q R S T U V W X Y Z

a b c d e f g h i j k l m

n o p q r s t u v w x y z

1 2 3 4 5 6 7 8 9 0

[! ? & @ $]

53 pt

SpeedFreek
Fontalicious Fonts, 1999
www.fontalicious.com

CD

RETROHEAVY FUTURE

Satellit

64 pt

ABCDEFGHI

JKLMNOPQR

STUVWXYZ

abcdefghijklm

nopqrstuvwxyz

1234567890

[!?@:;]

27 pt

Retroheavy Future
Cyclone Graphics, 1998
www.dafont.com

CD

SEEDS

Future

100 pt

abcdefghi

jklmnopqr

stuvwxyz

1234567890

(!?:;)

50 pt

Seeds
Matt Perkins, 1997
www.dafont.com

CD

FOLIO

Sie ist kräftig im Strich, stark in der Auszeichnung und hat ein eigenes Gesicht. Man spürt den frischen Wind der Folio und erkennt, wie lebendig eine Grotesk sein kann.

22 pt

ABCDEFGHI
JKLMNOPQR
STUVWXYZ
abcdefghijklm
nopqrstuvwxyz
äöü1234567890
(»!?&ß$£:;«)

40 pt

Folio
K. F. Bauer, W. Baum, 1957
www.linotype.com

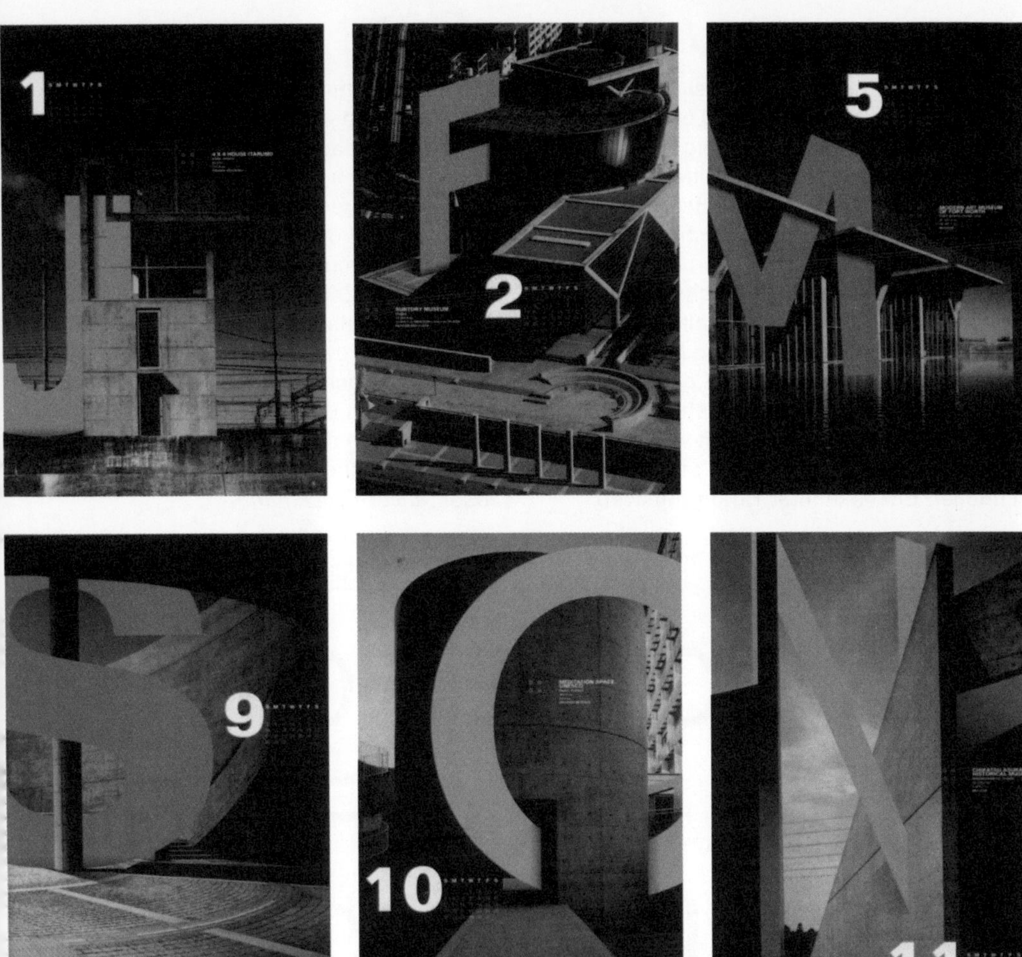

Student project
Sungjin Park, 2006

HELVETICA

Die Frage nach der Spaltenbreite ist nicht nur eine Frage der Gestaltung oder des Formats, ebenso bedeutsam ist die Frage der Leserlichkeit. Eine textliche Mitteilung soll vom Leser leicht und angenehm gelesen werden können. Dies hängt nicht zuletzt von der Grösse der Schrift, von der Länge der Zeilen und vom Zeilendurchschuss ab.

Die Drucksachen in Normalformat werden vom Auge gewöhnlich in einem Abstand von 30 bis 35 cm gelesen. Auf diese Distanz sollen die Schriftgrössen berechnet sein. Zu kleine wie zu grosse Schrift wird mit Anstrengung gelesen. Der Leser ermüdet schneller. Ein bekannter Erfahrungswert besagt, dass für einen längeren Text im Durchschnitt pro Zeile 7 Worte stehen sollen. Wenn wir auf eine Zeile 7 bis 10 Worte haben möchten, lässt sich die Länge der Zeile leicht errechnen. Damit das Schriftbild leicht und offen erscheint, haben wir den Zeilendurchschuss, also den vertikalen Abstand von Zeile zu Zeile, der Schriftgrösse angepasst, entsprechend zu bestimmen.

Ein weiteres Problem hat der Fotosatz mit sich gebracht, das des Buchstabenabstandes. Beim Bleisatz war der Buchstabenabstand durch die Kegelstärke bestimmt und ausgeglichen.
Josef Müller-Brockmann

10 pt

A B C D E F G H I
J K L M N O P Q R
S T U V W X Y Z
a b c d e f g h i j k l m
n o p q r s t u v w x y z
1 2 3 4 5 6 7 8 9 0
(ä ö ü ! ? & ß £ $ @ : ;)

40 pt

Helvetica
Max Miedinger, 1957
www.linotype.com

Helvetica Film + Fest
Flyer, Michael Bundscherer, 2007

CAMILLA

75 pt

ABCDEFGHIJKLM
NOPQRSTUVWXYZ
abcdefghijklm
nopqrstuvwxyz
1234567890
äöü!?@$€

55 pt

Camilla
Atrax, 2004
www.dafont.com

CD

QHYTSDAKX

Prototyp

145 pt

A B C D E F G H I J K L M

N O P Q R S T U V W X Y Z

a b c d e f g h i j k l m

n o p q r s t u v w x y z

1 2 3 4 5 6 7 8 9 0

(ä ö ü ! ? & @ € : ;)

55 pt

Qhytsdakx
Tepi Monkey Fonts, 2001
www.dafont.com

CD

MERCURY BLOB

code

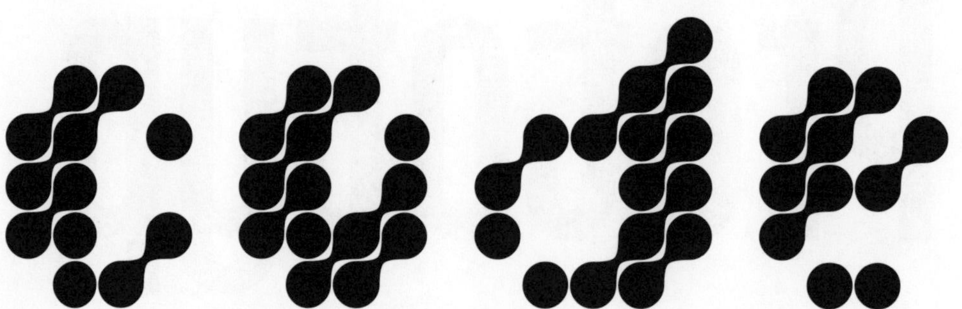

115 pt

abcdefghi
jklmnopqr
stuvwxyz
abcdefghij
klmnopqr
stuvwxyz
!?■,

35 pt

Mercury Blob
Matt Perkins, 1997
www.dafont.com

☞ CD

nonex ladyfitness
CD artwork
Fons Hickmann m23, 2000

ADDELECTRICCITY

Machine

80 pt

ABCDEFGHI
JKLMNOPQR
STUVWXYZ
abcdefghijklm
nopqrstuvwxyz
1234567890
(!?&$@:;)

39 pt

AddElectricCity
Atsushi Aoki, 1999
www.dafont.com

CD

BLACK WOLF

Cyber

And

Space

55 pt

ABCDEFGHI

JKLMNOPQR

STUVWXYZ

abcdefghijklm

nopqrstuvwxyz

1234567890

(äöü!?$@ no And :;)

38 pt

Black Wolf
Rich Gast, 1999
greywolfwebworks.home.insightbb.com

CD

Riesensprünge
Advertisement
Bild am Sonntag, 1960

ATOMICBOMB

STABHOCHSPRUNG

69 pt

ABCDEFGHI

JKLMNOPQR

STUVWXYZ

1234567890

:!?/,.

60 pt

AtomicBomb
David M. Debus, 1997
www.dafont.com

☞ CD

CIRCUIT

180 pt

ABCDEFGHI
JKLMNOPQR
STUVWXYZ
ABCDEFGHIJKLM
NOPQRSTUVWXYZ
1234567890
!?&@‡*;

38 pt

Circuit
1999
www.dafont.com

CD

OCR-A

Reader

92 pt

ABCDEFGHIJKLM
NOPQRSTUVWXYZ
abcdefghijklm
nopqrstuvwxyz
ÄÖÜ1234567890
(!?&@$*:;)

42 pt

OCR-A
Adrian Frutiger, 1968
www.linotype.com

CD

EUROSTILE

Mondlandung

70 pt

ABCDEFGHI
JKLMNOPQR
STUVWXYZ
abcdefghijklm
nopqrstuvwxyz
1234567890
(äöü!?&ß$£@:;)

43 pt

Eurostile
Aldo Novarese, 1962
www.linotype.com

Pool Event
Poster
Melchior Imboden, 2006

AS SEEN ON TV

Premiere

75 pt

ABCDEFGHI
JKLMNOPQR
STUVWXYZ
abcdefghijklm
nopqrstuvwxyz
1234567890
(äöü!?$:;)

33 pt

As seen on TV
Jakob Fischer, 2003
www.pizzadude.dk

t ≡ CD

SERPENTINE

Sender

95 pt

ABCDEFGHI
JKLMNOPQR
STUVWXYZ
abcdefghijklm
nopqrstuvwxyz
1234567890
(„äöü!?&£$")

40 pt

Serpentine
Dick Jensen, 1972
www.linotype.com

Mojo
Jim Parkinson
1960 | page 465

1968
—
1980

Flower Power

Cooper Black
Oswald Cooper
1921 | page 425

Varisystems phototypesetting machine, 1972

Flower Power and Revolt
Pop and Disco

c. 1968–1980

The seventies were marked by a longing for more emotional design. Playfulness returned, colours came back into fashion, sharp edges became soft and round. These forms were intended to romanticize and change all aspects of life – a holistic, ornamental and anti-technological aesthetic emerged, not unlike the Art Nouveau movement at the turn of the century. Type designers at the time did not however, take to it immediately. Their aesthetic models come not from within the typographic profession itself, but rather from youth subculture, the music scene or contemporary art.

The Doors
Poster, 1967

Flower Power and Revolt
Pop and Disco

c. 1968–1980

Frankfurter
Highlight
Bob Newman
1970 | page 462

Pinocchio
Dieter Steffmann
1994 | page 460

The letterforms were frequently inspired by fin de siècle style. They have a flat, dynamic, almost ornamental appearance. Idiosyncratic headline fonts emerged that were a mixture of Art Nouveau brushed and decorative scripts. Some resemble platform shoes and bulge out at the bottom, while others swell up, taking on the soft, rounded shape distinctive of the time. Sans-serif Grotesque fonts with rounded edges or with an artificial character were likewise the fashion, often in thick styles.

The limitations of hot-metal typesetting were removed by phototypesetting, and fonts could be enlarged, shrunk, distorted, compressed or widened with ease. Where previously it was impossible to reduce the spaces because of the metal sorts that accommodate them, it became a matter of utter simplicity, and as a result, narrower typefaces became popular.

The film *Saturday Night Fever* unleashed a worldwide craze disco that was reflected in the music, fashion and lifestyle of the young. This marked the start of John Travolta's career; and for typographers it was an excuse to reach deep into their bag of tricks. Typefaces took a variety of special effects including 3-D, mirror ball and gloss.

Typefaces

Cooper Black

Variants of Antiqua

The preference for soft, round forms in typography survives. Accordingly, the serifs of most variants of Antique are soft and round. Others make allusion to Art Nouveau.

Characteristics

Bauhaus

Sans-serif fonts with an artificial character

New type designs emerge that are modelled on the products of Elementary Typography and based on a purely constructed aesthetic. They are characterized by a geometric appearance.

Characteristics

FRANKFURTER

Sans-serif variants of Antiqua

Round sans-serif variants of Antique remained in fashion as well. Moreover, they were laden with effects such as gloss, hard shadows or 3-D.

Characteristics

Candice

Healdine scripts

Typical headline fonts of the seventies were forceful designs that would often swell at the bottom, exhibiting a 'platform shoe effect' or sweeping curves.

Characteristics

MOJO

Psychedelic scripts

These contemporary designs with psychedelic backgrounds are related artistically to the decorative fonts of Art Nouveau. They are often twisted into spiral shapes or distorted to hallucinatory effect.

Characteristics

Pump Triline

Disco scripts

The typical disco aesthetic in type design emerges through a linear construct, out of which most of the scripts of this species are put together. Gloss and disco ball effects are also popular.

Characteristics

Example:
Cooper Black
Oswald Cooper
1921 | page 425

Example:
Bauhaus
Edward Benguiat,
Victor Caruso
1975 | page 458

Example:
Frankfurter
Highlight
Bob Newman
1970 | page 462

Example:
Candice
Alan Meeks
1978 | page 418

Example:
Mojo
Jim Parkinson
1960 | page 465

Example:
Pump Triline
Corel Corporation
1992 | page 431

Characteristics

Typefaces

Art Nouveau scripts make a comeback. Not only are particular designs from the turn of the century – Eckmann, Hobo, Metropolitans, to name a few – rescued from the brink of obscurity, but a series of headline fonts are introduced that are clearly based on historical fonts. Furthermore, rounded scripts, with or without serifs, alphabets with line effects and constructed Grotesque scripts also enjoy a measure of popularity.

Text

Generally, scripts tend to be set in the thicker styles and (in headlines) all-caps. In these cases, a somewhat narrower gap between letters is preferred on the grounds that this would make for optimal legibility – a style made possible by phototype.

Illustrations, Effects and Colours

The usual motifs are hallucinatory distortions, twisted spirals and creatively exaggerated solarization effects. Colours are expressive, rich and varied. Illustrators use watercolours or an array of halftones. Peace symbols and other emblems of freedom are commonly used as ornaments.

BOTTLENECK

Plateausohle

90 pt

ABCDEFGHI
JKLMNOPQR
STUVWXYZ
abcdefghijklm
nopqrstuvwxyz
1234567890
(äöü!?&$€@:;)

44 pt

Bottleneck
Tony Wenman, 1972
www.linotype.com

PUPPYLIKE

Disco
Dance

100 pt

ABCDEFGHI
JKLMNOPQR
STUVWXYZ
abcdefghijklm
nopqrstuvwxyz
1234567890
(äöü!?&$:;)

40 pt

Puppylike
enStep Incorporated, 1996
www.dafont.com

CD

Chamber Brothers
Poster, 1967

BUTTERFIELD

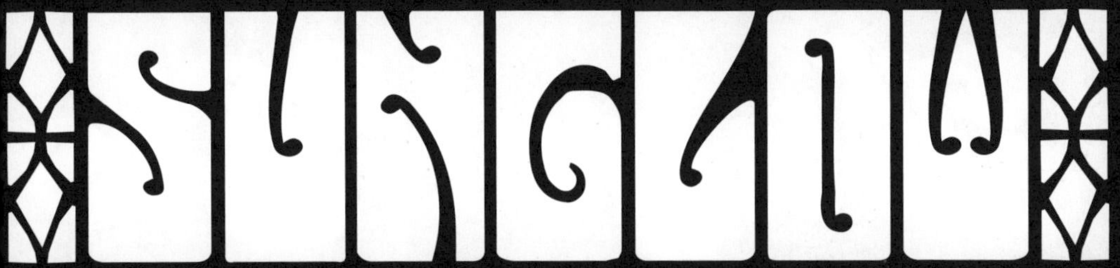

142 pt

ABCDEFGHIJKLM
NOPQRSTUVWXYZ

abcdefghi
jklmnopqr
stuvwxyz

57 pt

Butterfield
David Nalle, 2001
www.fontcraft.com

CD

CANDICE

Kugel Eis

90 pt

A B C D E F G H I
J K L M N O P Q R
S T U V W X Y Z
a b c d e f g h i j k l m
n o p q r s t u v w x y z
ä ö ü 1 2 3 4 5 6 7 8 9 0
(„ ! ? & fi fl ß £ $ * : ; ")

41 pt

Candice
Alan Meeks, 1978
www.linotype.com

ITC SOUVENIR

Der rote Apfelbackensommer.
Der ocker Strandsommer.
Der himmelhellblaue Sonnensommer.
Der orangene Blumensommer.
Der gelbe Kornsommer.

15 pt

ABCDEFGHI
JKLMNOPQR
STUVWXYZ
abcdefghijklm
nopqrstuvwxyz
1234567890
(„ ! ? & fi fl ß £ $ * “)

40 pt

ITC Souvenir
Edward Benguiat, 1972
www.linotype.com

ITC BENGUIAT

Und plötzlich ist Farbverständigung möglich.
Plötzlich sprechen alle eine Sprache, die über Farben
sprechen: Der Auftraggeber und der Gestalter, der
Gestalter und der Drucker, der Drucker und
der Druckfarbenhersteller.

15 pt

A B C D E F G H I
J K L M N O P Q R
S T U V W X Y Z
a b c d e f g h i j k l m
n o p q r s t u v w x y z
1 2 3 4 5 6 7 8 9 0
(ä ö ü ! ? & ß $ £)

42 pt

ITC Benguiat
Edward Benguiat, 1977
www.linotype.com

Southern Sessions
Flyer
C100 Purple Haze, 2005

HAWTHORN

Ein deutlich ausgeprägter Hang zum Tragischen, stark gefühlsbetont, Neurotiker, Einzelgänger.

40 pt

A B C D E F G H I
J K L M N O P Q R
S T U V W X Y Z
a b c d e f g h i j k l m
n o p q r s t u v w x y z
ä ö ü 1 2 3 4 5 6 7 8 9 0
(„ ! ? & ß £ $ * : ; “)

43 pt

Hawthorn
Mike Daines, 1968
www.linotype.com

ITC TIFFANY HEAVY

Juwelier

75 pt

ABCDEFGHI
JKLMNOPQR
STUVWXYZ
abcdefghijklm
nopqrstuvwxyz
1234567890
(äöü!?&ß£$)

36 pt

ITC Tiffany Heavy
Edward Benguiat, 1974
www.linotype.com

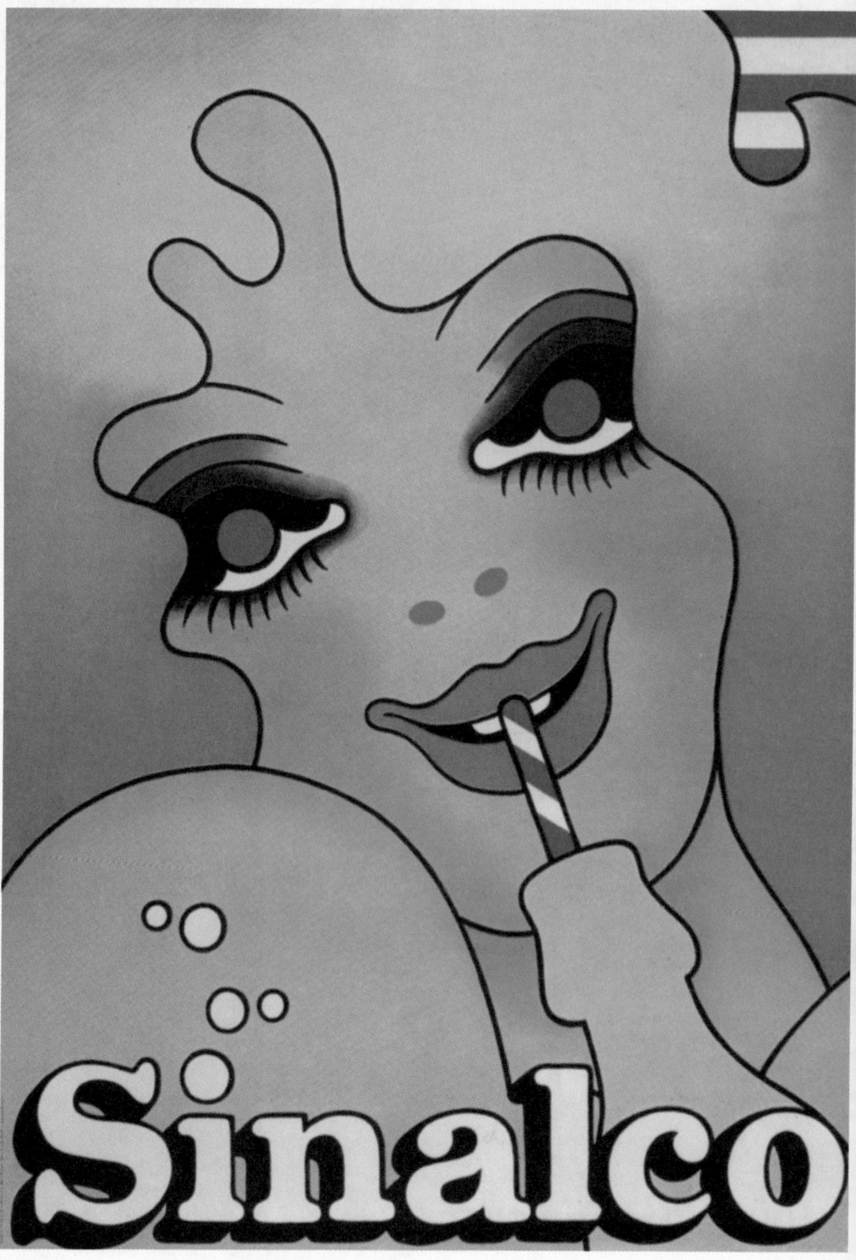

Sinalco
Poster
Willi Rieser, 1972

COOPER BLACK

Softdrink

75 pt

ABCDEFGHI
JKLMNOPQR
STUVWXYZ
abcdefghijklm
nopqrstuvwxyz
äöü1234567890
(!?&fiflß$€@)

37 pt

Cooper Black
Oswald Cooper, 1921
www.linotype.com

ITC BENGUIAT GOTHIC

Sein Element ist das Feuer. Der Pulverfaßtyp, der mit Freuden bereit ist, jederzeit hochzugehen. Dabei ein energischer, vitaler, dynamischer Arbeiter. Durchsetzungskräftig, überzeugend, produktiv, progressiv, aggressiv.

15 pt

ABCDEFGHI
JKLMNOPQR
STUVWXYZ
abcdefghijklm
nopqrstuvwxyz
1234567890
(äöü!?&ß£$:;)

43 pt

ITC Benguiat Gothic
Edward Benguiat, 1979
www.linotype.com

RONDA

Tankstelle

90 pt

ABCDEFGHI
JKLMNOPQR
STUVWXYZ
abcdefghijklm
nopqrstuvwxyz
1234567890
(äöü!?&ß£$:;)

41 pt

Ronda
Herb Lubalin, 1970
www.linotype.com

MADONNA

PROMO

105 pt

ABCDEFG
HIJKLMNO
PQRSTUV
WXYZ

60 pt

Madonna
Romulo Genova, 2007
www.dafont.com

[illegible] CD

Madonna
CD cover
Giovanni Bianco, 2005

BLIPPO

Dancer

110 pt

ABCDEFGHI
JKLMNOPQR
STUVWXYZ
abcdefghijklm
nopqrstuvwxyz
1234567890
(äöü!?&ß£$:;)

40 pt

Blippo
Fotostar, 1970
www.linotype.com

PUMP TRILINE

Studio

120 pt

ABCDEFGHI
JKLMNOPQR
STUVWXYZ
abcdefghijklm
nopqrſstuvwxyz
1234567890
(äöü!?&£$:;)

42 pt

Pump Triline
Corel Corporation, 1992
www.linotype.com

PARIS 1970 TAKE-OVER! THE WORD IS FREE!

The NEWS... color—burgundy, cinnamon, rust, French-navy blue, layered one over the other. The fabric, knit. Opposite left: Multicolor cape knitted and fringed like a crazy cocoon! Burgundy dress—banded at the hem in cinnamon, wrapped at the neck in a muffler of red, purple, green. Head wrapped in violent spring green. Center: Violet shorts and pullover, green double cape—dare color... red boots, electric blue stockings—head of multicolors from green to rust to violet. Right: Blue cape over a coat, to-the-ankle rust skirt—jacquard short-sleeved sweater over cinnamon long-sleeved sweater—muffled and capped in rust. All by Dorothée Bis for Benson and Partners. Boots, left, Yves Saint Laurent at Lord & Taylor, Bloomingdale's. Boots, center and right, Charles Jourdan. Makeup on these 8 pages by Astarté. For additional merchandise information see page 76.

Essences of Paris You're beautiful—let the world know it!... ready-to-wear—pared down to essentials. Build on color... daring! Proud is the message—to fling a cape over your shoulders, to stride. It's you that counts... that's where the power is!

'Paris 1970 Take-Over!'

Paris magazine, 1970

AKKA

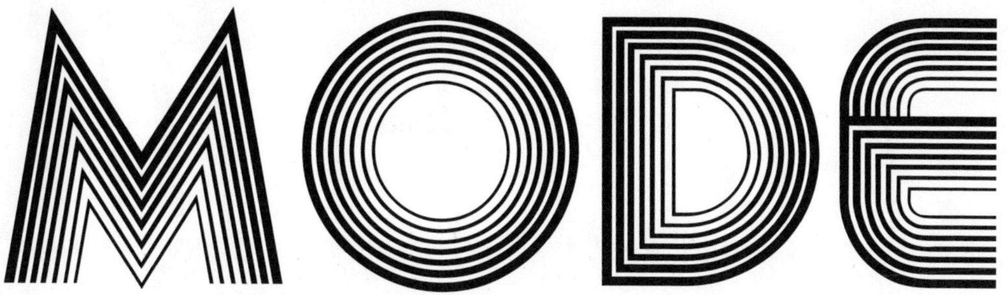

130 pt

ABCDEFGHI
JKLMNOPQR
STUVWXYZ
1234567890
(!?&$:;)

50 pt

Akka
2007
www.dafont.com

☞ CD

SF GROOVE MACHINE

BODY AND SOUL

100 / 52 pt

ABCDEFGHIJKLM
NOPQRSTUVWXYZ
ABCDEFGHIJKLM
NOPQRSTUVWXYZ
ÄÖÜ1234567890
[„!?€$@*:;“]

50 pt

SF Groove Machine
ShyFoundry, 1999
www.shyfoundry.com

CD

SPACEBEACH

nightlife

140 pt

ABCDEFGHIJKLM

NOPQRSTUVWXYZ

abcdefghijklm

nopqrstuvwxyz

äöü1234567890

(! ? ¢ $ £ @ $ ❀ ❀ ❀)

VELCRO

Funki

180 pt

ABCDEFGHIJKLM

NOPQRSTUVWXYZ

abcdefghijklm

nopqrstuvwxyz

äöü1234567890

(! ? fi fl $ € @)

52 pt

Velcro
Fontalicious Fonts, 2002
www.fontalicious.com

CD

Soul Explosion
Flyer, 2008

BUSTER

DIMENSION

65 pt

A B C D E F G

H I J K L M N O

P Q R S T U V

W X Y Z Ä Ö Ü

1 2 3 4 5 6 7 8 9 0

50 pt

Buster
Tony Wenman, 1972
www.linotype.com

ITC PIONEER

PORNOBALKEN

60 pt

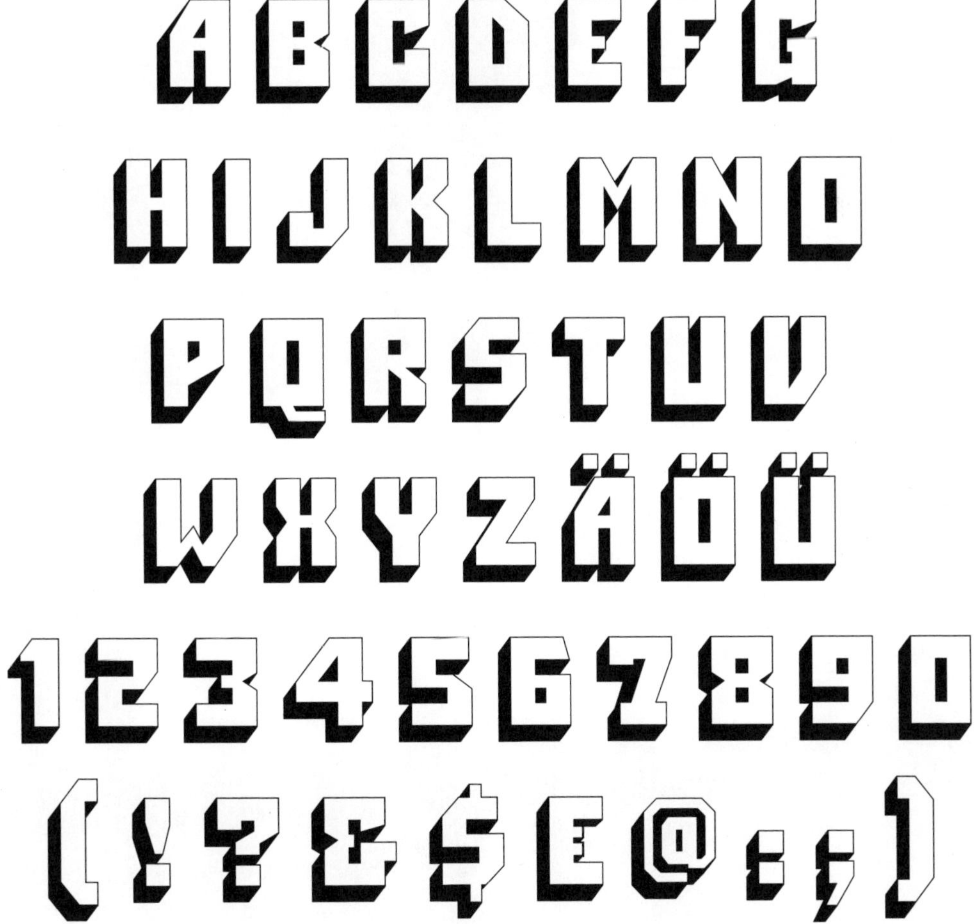

50 pt

ITC Pioneer
Ronnie Bonder, Tom Carnase, 1970
www.linotype.com

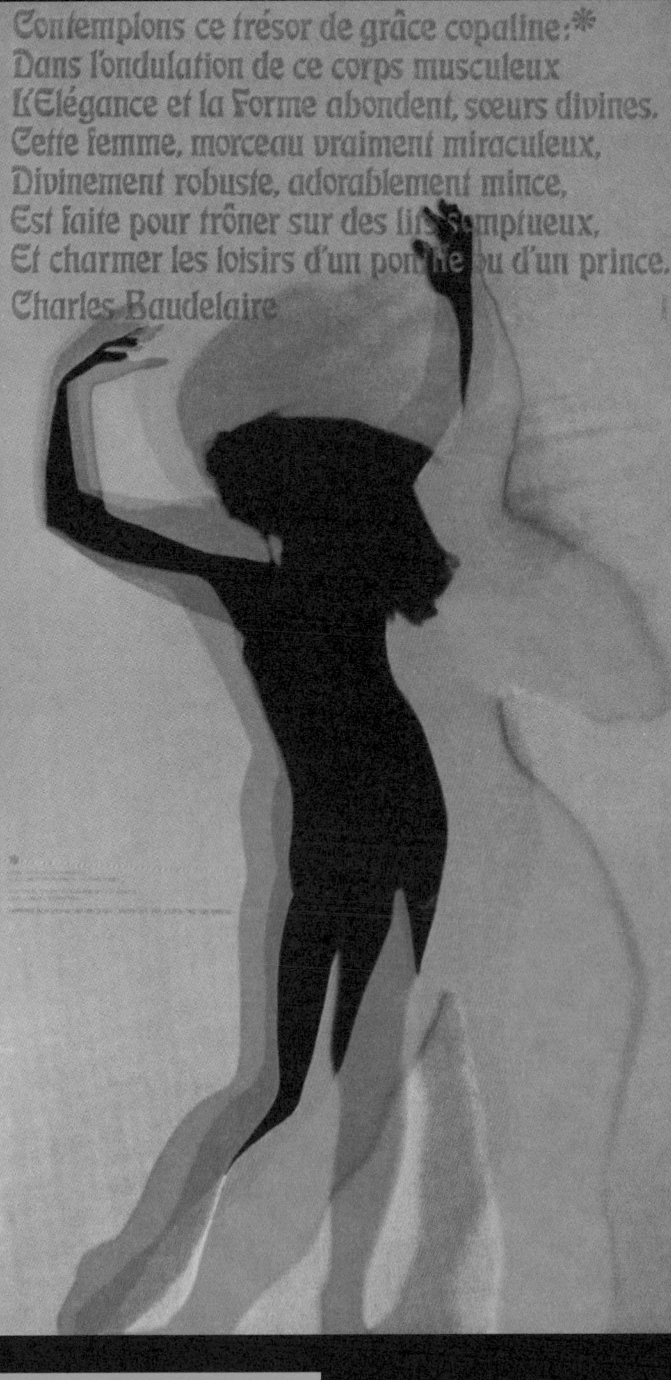

Copaline
Poster
Jacques Richez, 1971

KEEP ON TRUCKIN

Kommune

80 pt

ABCDEFGHI
JKLMNOPQR
STUVWXYZ
abcdefghijklm
nopqrstuvwxyz
1234567890
(!?&ß£$€@*:;)

38 pt

Keep on Truckin
Brad O. Nelson, 2003
www.fontdiner.com

CD

GOSOUL

Love &
Peace

80 / 130 pt

ABCDEFGHI
JKLMNOPQR
STUVWXYZ
abcdefghijklm
nopqrstuvwxyz
1234567890
(!?&$✤☮✿:;❤)

38 pt

GoSoul
Grass Onions, 1999
www.dafont.com

CD

VICTOR MOSCOSO

SHAKE

160 pt

ABCDEFGHI
JKLMNOPQR
STUVWXYZ

ABCDEFGHIJKLM
NOPQRSTUVWXYZ
1234567890
(!?&£$€@:;)

40 pt

Victor Moscoso
Keith Bates, 2006
www.k-type.com

CD

LAZYBONES

Agent

140 pt

A B C D E F G H I
J K L M N O P Q
R S T U V W X Y Z
a b c d e f g h i j k l m
n o p q r s t u v w x y z
ä ö ü 1 2 3 4 5 6 7 8 9 0
(„ ! ? & ß $ * : ; “)

42 pt

Lazybones
Letraset Design Studio, 1972
www.linotype.com

James Bond
Book covers
Jon Gray, 2008

LORRAINE SCRIPT

Lustmolch

120 pt

A B C D E F G H I
J K L M N O P Q R
S T U V W X Y Z
a b c d e f g h i j k l m
n o p q r s t u v w x y z
ä ö ü 1 2 3 4 5 6 7 8 9 0
(! ? & ﬁ ﬂ ß £ $ @)

41 pt

Lorraine Script
Bob Alonso, 2000
www.myfonts.com

JULIA SCRIPT

Freie Liebe

100 pt

ABCDEFGHI
JKLMNOPQR
STUVWXYZ
abcdefghijklm
nopqrstuvwxyz
äöü1234567890
(„!?&ß£$*:;“)

41 pt

Julia Script
David Harris, 1983
www.linotype.com

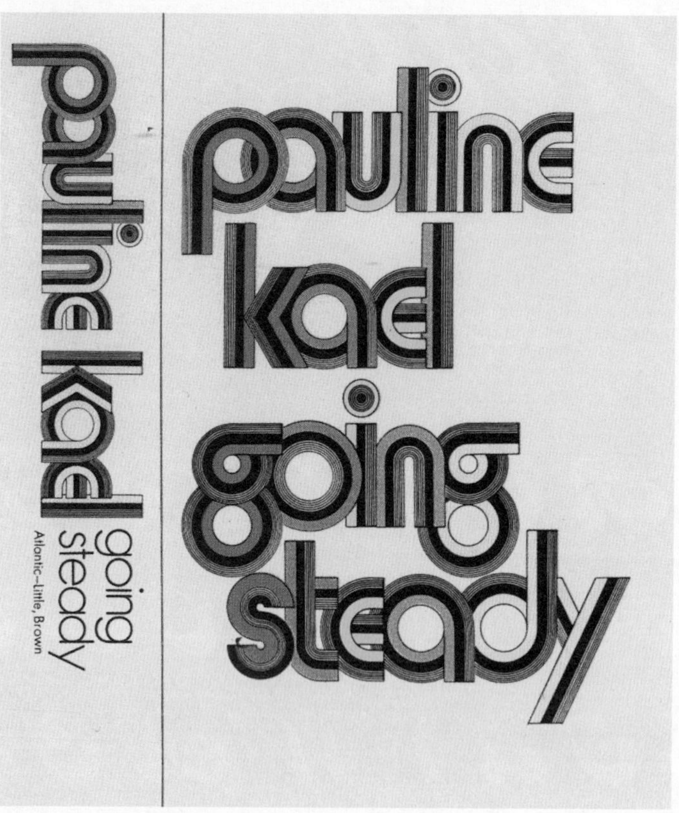

Going Steady
Book cover
Push Pin Studio, 1972

DISCO 1

ready.steady.go

120 pt

abcdefg

hijklmnopq

rstuvwxyz

1234567890

äöü:.

90 pt

Disco 1
Fenotype Typefaces, 2002
www.fenotype.com

CD

ALBA SUPER

115 pt

ABCDEFGHI
JKLMNOPQR
STUVWXYZ
abcdefghijklm
nopqrstuvwxyz
1234567890
(äöü!? and ß ¿ €@:;)

35 pt

Alba Super
Fontalicious Fonts, 2001
www.fontalicious.com

☞ CD

OCTOPUSS

Tentakel

105 pt

ABCDEFGHI
JKLMNOPQR
STUVWXYZ
abcdefghijklm
nopqrstuvwxyz
äöü1234567890
(„!?&ß$£:;“)

43 pt

Octopuss
Colin Brignall, 1970
www.linotype.com

TANGO

Novelle

140 pt

A B C D E F G H I
J K L M N O P Q R
S T U V W X Y Z
a b c d e f g h i j k l m
n o p q r s t u v w x y z
1 2 3 4 5 6 7 8 9 0
(ä ö ü ! ? & ß $ £)

50 pt

Tango
Colin Brignall, 1974
www.linotype.com

A Fraction of the Whole
Book cover
Nathan Burton, 2008

STILLA

Lava
Lampe

70 pt

ABCDEFGHI
JKLMNOPQR
STUVWXYZ
abcdefghijklm
nopqrstuvwxyz
äöü1234567890
(!?&ß£$€:;)

30 pt

Stilla
François Boltana, 1973
www.linotype.com

FLAMENCO INLINE

Playback

100 pt

ABCDEFGHI
JKLMNOPQR
STUVWXYZ
abcdefghijklm
nopqrstuvwxyz
äöü1234567890
(„!?&ß£$€:;“)

41 pt

Flamenco Inline
Tony Geddes, 1979
www.linotype.com

Nijinsky, der Gott des Tanzes
Book cover
Willy Fleckhaus, 1974

ITC AVANT GARDE GOTHIC

Biografie

100 pt

ABCDEFGHIJKLM

NOPQRSTUVWXYZ

abcdeefghijklm

nopqrstuvwxyz

äöü1234567890

(!?&© LA ST TT st ff fi ß $ €)

35 pt

ITC Avant Garde Gothic
Herb Lubalin, Tom Carnase, 1970
www.linotype.com

ITC BAUHAUS

Weimar

95 pt

ABCDEFGHI
JKLMNOPQR
STUVWXYZ
abcdefghijklm
nopqrstuvwxyz
äöü1234567890
(„!?&ß$£:;")

40 pt

ITC Bauhaus
Edward Benguiat, Victor Caruso, 1975
www.linotype.com

ITC ERAS

Translator

95 pt

ABCDEFGHI
JKLMNOPQR
STUVWXYZ
abcdefghijklm
nopqrstuvwxyz
1234567890
(äöü!?&ß$£@)

43 pt

ITC Eras
Albert Boton, 1976
www.linotype.com

PINOCCHIO

ELEFANT

95 pt

ABCDEFGH

IJKLMNOPQR

STUVWXYZ

1234567890

ÄÖÜ!?&$£:;

50 pt

Pinocchio
Dieter Steffmann, 1994
www.steffmann.de

t CD

The White Stripes
Poster
Justin Hampton, 2003

FRANKFURTER HIGHLIGHT

BUBBLE

115 pt

ABCDEFGHI

JKLMNOPQR

STUVWXYZ

1234567890

(» ! ? £ $: ; «)

52 pt

Frankfurter Highlight
Bob Newman, 1970
www.linotype.com

GREASE

Schmiere

80 pt

ABCDEFGHI
JKLMNOPQR
STUVWXYZ
abcdefghijklm
nopqrstuvwxyz
1234567890
(„!?&$£@:;“)

36 pt

Grease
Rafael Dinner, 1996
www.dafont.com

CD

Jefferson Airplane, Grateful Dead
gig poster
James H. Gardner, 1967

MOJO

FESTIVAL

170 pt

ABCDEFGH

IJKLMNOPQR

STUVWXYZ

1234567890

ÄÖÜ!?&$£€

70 pt

Mojo
Jim Parkinson, 1960
www.adobe.com/type

BELL BOTTOM LASER

Superheld

95 pt

A B C D E F G H I
J K L M N O P Q R
S T U V W X Y Z
a b c d e f g h i j k l m
n o p q r s t u v w x y z
1 2 3 4 5 6 7 8 9 0
(! ? & $: ;)

40 pt

Bell Bottom Laser
1991
www.dafont.com

CD

COASTER

Comic

140 pt

ABCDEFGHI
JKLMNOPQR
STUVWXYZ
abcdefghijklm
nopqrstuvwxyz
1234567890
(äöü!?&$:;)

43 pt

Coaster
Dieter Steffmann, 2001
www.steffmann.de

CD

BABY KRUFFY

CLUB

170 pt

ABCDEFGHI
JKLMNOPQR
STUVWXYZ
abcdefghijklm
nopqrstuvwxyz
äöü1234567890
(!?$&$@*)

38 pt

Baby Kruffy
Fontalicious Fonts, 1999
www.fontalicious.com

CD

The Fever
Flyer, c. 2008

BAVEUSE

FREAK

95 pt

aBCDEFGHI

JKLMNOPQR

STUVWXYZ

1234567890

äÖÜ!?&ß£€@

40 pt

Baveuse
Ray Larabie, 2000
www.larabiefonts.com

CD

FLORALIES

105 pt

a B C D e F G H I

J K L M N O P Q R

S T U V W X Y Z

a B C D e F G h i J K L M N

o P Q R S t U V W X Y Z

1 2 3 4 5 6 7 8 9 0

- . ! ? & $: ;

37 pt

Floralies
Keith Field, 1994
www.dafont.com

☞ CD

The 13th Floor Elevators
Record sleeve
John Cleveland, 1967

HENDRIX

PSYCHE

120 pt

ABCDE

FGHI

JKLMN

OPQR

STUVW

60 pt

Hendrix,
David Nalle, 2002
www.fontcraft.com

CD

HYPMOTIZIN

110 pt

A B C D E F G H I

J K L M N O P Q R

S T U V W X Y Z

A B C D E F G H I J K L M

N O P Q R S T U V W X Y Z

1 2 3 4 5 6 7 8 9 0

(! ? & $ @ " * : ;)

45 pt

Hypmotizin
Rich Gast, 1999
greywolfwebworks.home.insightbb.com

☞ CD

STARBURST

BROKE

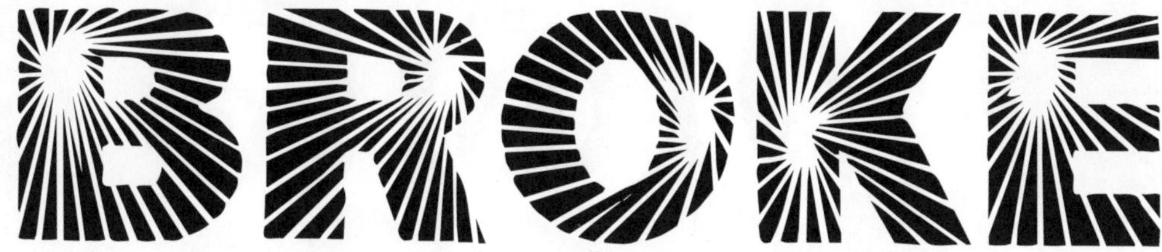

90 pt

ABCDEFGHI

JKLMNOPQR

STUVWXYZ

1234567890

!?&$:;

43 pt

Starburst
David Rakowski, 1990
www.dafont.com

☞ CD

MUSICALS

MU𝄞IC

95 / 170 pt

ABCDEFGH

IJKLMNOPQR

STUVWXYZ

1234567890

♪ ♫ 𝄞 ! ? $ @ *

50 pt

Musicals
Brad O. Nelson, 2000
www.braineaters.com

t . CD

Pluxus
CD cover
Burnfield, 2002

ITC AMERICAN TYPEWRITER

I love NewYork

85 pt

ABCDEFGHI
JKLMNOPQR
STUVWXYZ
abcdefghijklm
nopqrstuvwxyz
äöü1234567890
(„!?&ß£$€“)

40 pt

ITC American Typewriter
Edward Benguiat, Tony Stan, Joel Kaden, 1974
www.linotype.com

HARLOW

Discothek

100 pt

A B C D E F G H I
J K L M N O P Q R
S T U V W X Y Z
a b c d e f g h i j k l m
n o p q r s t u v w x y z
ä ö ü 1 2 3 4 5 6 7 8 9 0
(» ! ? & fi fl ß £ $: ; «)

42 pt

Harlow
Colin Brignall, 1977/79
www.linotype.com

ChicagoFLF
Richard A. Ware
1990–92 | page 492

1975
—
1990

Achtziger
Jahre

Apple's first Macintosh, 1984

Anything goes

Steadmanesque
Foxx Nolte
2003 | page 513

Walkman, Rubik's Cube and Gen X *Postmodern and Punk*

c. 1975–1990

Graphic design and typography became dogma free. Instead of seeking the modern in a single, solitary visual form, a plurality of styles and influences was celebrated. This was accompanied also by a rebellion against functionalism. Forms were laden with semantic allusions that go beyond their primary function: they used quotation, they were ironic, they used collage. While the champions of modernity frequently criticize commercial mass culture, the postmodern itself became the dominant culture. Meanwhile, there was growth in the importance of design for its own sake, and the eighties achieved the status of the 'design decade.'

i-D
Magazine cover
August 1985

Walkman, Rubik's Cube and Gen X
Postmodern and Punk

c. 1975–1990

Design of this period is marked by a desire to use existing ideas and forms to create something new. Thus, the forms of earlier decades are quoted, revived and mixed together. New typefaces are intentionally hard to categorize. As in the Art Deco period, several designs demonstrate a delight in experimentation with geometrical forms. At the same time Chicago, Apple's first system font, is developed and also completely different designs that sustain the disco style of the seventies.

Meanwhile, punk culture develops its own unique typographical expression: scribbling, collages formed from newspaper type, fragments pasted together, ripped and painted over or typed out and copied. Randomness becomes an essential element of design. This 'damaged' look can be exaggerated through the process of production: posters are simply copied or silk screened in basements and garages and then posted illegally on lamp-posts and walls.

Typefaces

Trash fonts (punk)

Characteristics

variex

The typefaces of the eighties decisively detached themselves from functionalism. The letterforms are laden with allusion that goes beyond their function.

Variants of Antiqua

Characteristics

SLIPSTREAM

Some display fonts represent the further development of seventies disco style. Lines and other effects remain characteristic of this style.

Headline scripts

Characteristics

With the advent of digitalization, several designs are aimed at breaking all the rules of traditional typography, almost to the point of illegibility. These scripts experiment with two key elements: error and accident.

Postmodern scripts

Characteristics

SINALOA

These type designs, which are constructed out of purely geometric forms, make contact with the stylistic characteristics of Art Deco. An idiosyncratic typeface is achieved by eliminating counters.

Geo-scripts

Characteristics

Senator

The first pixelated fonts sprang from the triumph of the personal computer in design offices. The technical limitations are consciously used to aesthetic ends.

Pixelated scripts

Characteristics

Moksha

Punk posters were not typeset but actually scribbled or collaged. Thanks to PostScript, today we have countless fonts whose design makes at least some contact with them.

Characteristics

Example: Variex
Rudy VanderLans
Zuzana Licko
1988 | page 527

Example: Slipstream
Letraset
1985 | page 539

Example: Scratched Out
Pierredi Sciullo
1992 | page 519

Example: Sinaloa
Rosemarie Tissi
1974 | page 534

Example: Senator
Zuzana Licko
1988 | page 503

Example: Moksha
Eduardo Recife
2007 | page 516

Typefaces

Mainstream production is partial to the forms of Art Deco. Circles, triangles and squares are used decoratively or to construct letter-like forms and colophons. Appropriately, people turn to Grotesque fonts in the characteristic style of Futura or Avantgarde. After thc thicker styles of the seventies, extra-light styles are employed. Sometimes these are combined with brushed and poster scripts.

Punk typography used handwritten, typewritten or collaged fonts.

Text

Whether tilted, diagonal or circular, everything is allowed. Form and figure complement the compositional feel with geometric forms in editorial design.

Ornaments

Geometrical forms, lines and waves were frequently used for ornamentation. Moreover, all manner of historical props were used; even kitsch and parody were not avoided. Trendy neon colours and the basic process colours cyan, magenta and yellow were in fashion. Colours of the punk aesthetic were frequently limited to black-and-white, greyscale and red.

PAGE
Magazine cover
Gabriele Günder, 1989

MODULA

Editorial Design

115 pt

A B C D E F G H I J K L M

N O P Q R S T U V W X Y Z

a b c d e f g g h i j k l

m n o p q r s t u v w x y z

ä ö ü 1 2 3 4 5 6 7 8 9 0

(! ? & fi fl ß $ @ : ;)

60 pt

Modula
Zuzana Licko, 1985
www.emigre.com

ITC OFFICINA SANS

Bürokraft

70 pt

ABCDEFGHI
JKLMNOPQR
STUVWXYZ
abcdefghijklm
nopqrstuvwxyz
1234567890
(äöü!?&ß£$@:;)

43 pt

ITC Officina Sans
Erik Spiekermann, 1990
www.linotype.com

ROTIS SANS SERIF

Küchenhilfe

70 pt

A B C D E F G H I
J K L M N O P Q R
S T U V W X Y Z
a b c d e f g h i j k l m
n o p q r s t u v w x y z
1 2 3 4 5 6 7 8 9 0
(ä ö ü ! ? & ß £ $ @)

42 pt

Rotis Sans Serif
Otl Aicher, 1989
www.linotype.com

BLUR

Print error

140 pt

ABCDEFGHI
JKLMNOPQR
STUVWXYZ
abcdefghijklm
nopqrstuvwxyz
äöü1234567890
(!?&ﬁﬂß£$@:;)

46 pt

Blur
Neville Brody, 1992
www.fontfont.com

TEMPLATE GOTHIC

Young Urban Professional

70 pt

ABCDEFGHI
JKLMNOPQR
STUVWXYZ
abcdefghijklm
nopqrstuvwxyz
äöü1234567890
(!?&fiflß£$at:;)

36 pt

Template Gothic
Barry Deck, 1990
www.emigre.com

CHICAGOFLF

Macintosh

70 pt

ABCDEFGHI
JKLMNOPQR
STUVWXYZ
abcdefghijklm
nopqrstuvwxyz
äöü1234567890
(!?&ß£$@:;)

36 pt

ChicagoFLF
Richard A. Ware, 1990–92
www.fontstock.net

CD

ISONORM 3098

Standard

100 pt

ABCDEFGHI
JKLMNOPQR
STUVWXYZ
abcdefghijklm
nopqrstuvwxyz
1234567890
(äöü!?&ß£$@:;)

45 pt

Isonorm 3098
International Standard Org., 1980
www.linotype.com

DEMOCRATICA

wie ihr werk
das Licht der welt
erblickt

50 pt

A B C D E F G H I
J K L M N O P Q R
S T U V W X Y Z
a b c d e f g h i j k l m
n o p q r s t u v w x y z
1 2 3 4 5 6 7 8 9 0
(ä ö ü ! ? & ß £ $ @ : ;)

45 pt

Democratica
Miles Newlyn, 1991
www.emigre.com

ROTIS SEMI SERIF

Eine Idee zu haben, ist nicht teuer.
Sie kostet zwar einiges an Überlegung,
ansonsten aber nur Papier
und ein paar Zentimeter Bleistift.

20 pt

A B C D E F G H I
J K L M N O P Q R
S T U V W X Y Z
a b c d e f g h i j k l m
n o p q r s t u v w x y z
1 2 3 4 5 6 7 8 9 0
(ä ö ü ! ? & ß £ $ @)

42 pt

Rotis Semi Serif
Otl Aicher, 1988
www.linotype.com

LUNATIX

Rundgang

90 pt

ABCDEFGHI
JKLMNOPQR
STUVWXYZ
abcdefghijklm
nopqrstuvwxyz
1234567890
(äöü!?&ß£$a:;)

42 pt

Lunatix
Zuzana Licko, 1988
www.emigre.com

ULTRABRONZO

ROHBAU

95 pt

ABCDEFGHI
JKLMNOPQR
STUVWXYZ

ABCDEFGHIJKLM
NOPQRSTUVWXYZ
1234567890
(ÄÖÜ!?&ß£$@:;)

37 pt

UltraBronzo
Rick Valicenti, 1992
www.vilg.com

ARENA
Magazine cover
Neville Brody, 1988

INSIGNIA

Bunker

120 pt

ABCDEFGHI
JKLMNOPQR
STUVWXYZ
abcdefghijklm
nopqrstuvwxyz
1234567890
äöü!?&ﬁﬂß£$@

44 pt

Insignia
Neville Brody, 1989
www.linotype.com

CITIZEN

Ecken und Kanten

80 pt

ABCDEFGHI
JKLMNOPQR
STUVWXYZ
abcdefghijklm
nopqrstuvwxyz
äöü1234567890
(!?&fiflß£$@)

40 pt

Citizen
Zuzana Licko, 1986
www.emigre.com

TRIPLEX

Kurvenreich

80 pt

ABCDEFGHI
JKLMNOPQR
STUVWXYZ
abcdefghijklm
nopqrstuvwxyz
äöü1234567890
(!?&fiflß£$@:;)

45 pt

Triplex
Zuzana Licko, 1989
www.emigre.com

OBLONG

Pixelschubse

115 pt

A B C D E F G H I J K L M

N O P Q R S T U V W X Y Z

a b c d e f g h i j k l m

n o p q r s t u v w x y z

1 2 3 4 5 6 7 8 9 0

[ä ö ü ! ? & ß £ $ @ : ;]

60 pt

Oblong
Rudy VanderLans, Zuzana Licko, 1988
www.emigre.com

SENATOR

Konsulat

120 pt

ABCDEFGHIJKLM
NOPQRSTUVWXYZ
abcdefghijklm
nopqrstuvwxyz
1234567890
(äöü!?&ß£$¢:;)

50 pt

Senator
Zuzana Licko, 1988
www.emigre.com

ARBITRARY

Desktop

120 pt

ABCDEFGHI
JKLMNOPQR
STUVWXYZ
abcdefghijklm
nopqrstuvwxyz
1234567890
(äöü!?&ß£$@:;)

40 pt

Arbitrary
Barry Deck, 1990
www.emigre.com

MATRIX

Was ist, was bringt und was kostet
das Desktop Publishing? Noch hat Pionier
Apple die Nase weit vorn – doch die
Konkurrenz wacht auf.

20 pt

A B C D E F G H I
J K L M N O P Q R
S T U V W X Y Z
a b c d e f g h i j k l m
n o p q r s t u v w x y z
1 2 3 4 5 6 7 8 9 0
(ä ö ü ! ? & ß £ $ @ : ;)

49 pt

Matrix
Zuzana Licko, 1986
www.emigre.com

KEEDY SANS

Partyflyer

75 pt

ABCDEFGHi
JKLMNOPQR
STUVWXYZ
abcdefghijklm
nopqrstuvwxyz
1234567890
(!?&ß$£@*:;)

40 pt

Keedy Sans
Jeffery Keedy, 1990
www.emigre.com

Basement Jaxx
CD cover
Big Active, c.2000

DEAD HISTORY

Anything goes

50 / 100 pt

ABCDEFGHI
JKLMNOPQR
STUVWXYZ
abcdefghijklm
nopqrstuvwxyz
1234567890
(äöü!?&ß£$@:;)

40 pt

Dead History
P. Scott Makela, 1990
www.emigre.com

ENTROPY

HYBRID

110 pt

A B C D E F G H I

J K L M N O P Q R

S T U V W X Y Z

1 2 3 4 5 6 7 8 9 0

(! ? & ß £ $ @ : ;)

Ä Ö Ü

45 pt

Entropy
Stephen Farrell, 1993
www.t26.com

Théâtre National

Poster

Grapus, 1982

SMACK

Nuckelflasche

75 pt

A B C D E F G H I
J K L M N O P Q R
S T U V W X Y Z
a b c d e f g h i j k l m
n o p q r s t u v w x y z
ä ö ü 1 2 3 4 5 6 7 8 9 0
! ? & fi fl ß £ € @ : ;

41 pt

Smack
Jill Bell, 1995
www.linotype.com

BRONX

Breakdance

63 pt

ABCDEFGHI
JKLMNOPQR
STUVWXYZ
abcdefghijklm
nopqrstuvwxyz
1234567890
(äöü!?&ß£$:;)

37 pt

Bronx
David Quay, 1986
www.linotype.com

STEADMANESQUE

120 pt

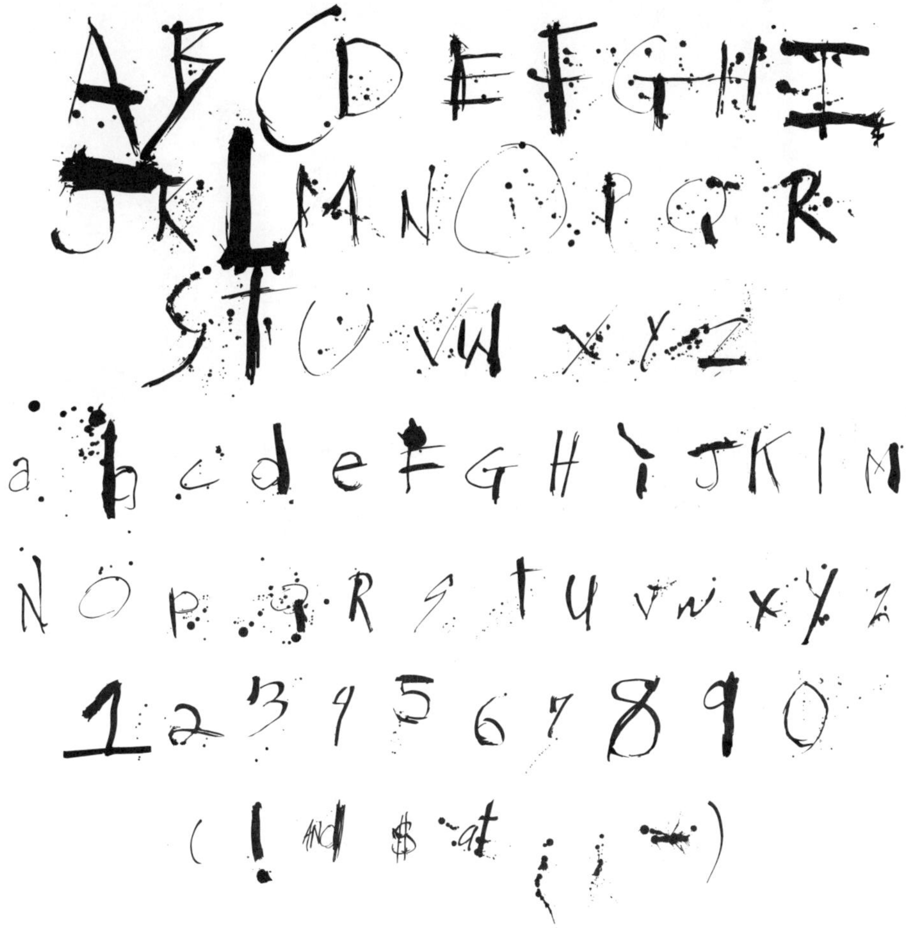

ABCDEFGHI
JKLMNOPQR
STUVWXYZ

abcdefghijklm
nopqrstuvwxyz
1234567890
(!&$@,;-)

35 pt

Steadmanesque
Foxx Nolte, 2003
www.dafont.com

CD

Sex Pistols
Record sleeve
Jamie Reid, 1977

BROKEN 15

Lösegeld

140 pt

ABCDEFGHI
JKLMNOPQR
STUVWXYZ
abcdefghijklm
nopqrstuvwxyz
äöü1234567890
(!?&ß£$@)

50 pt

Broken 15
Eduardeo Recife, 2001
www.misprintedtype.com

MOKSHA

Plakatieren Verboten!

90 pt

ABCDEFGHI
JKLMNOPQR
STUVWXYZ
abcdefghijklm
nopqrstuvwxyz
1234567890
(!?&ß$£€@*:;)

40 pt

Moksha
Eduardo Recife, 2007
www.misprintedtype.com

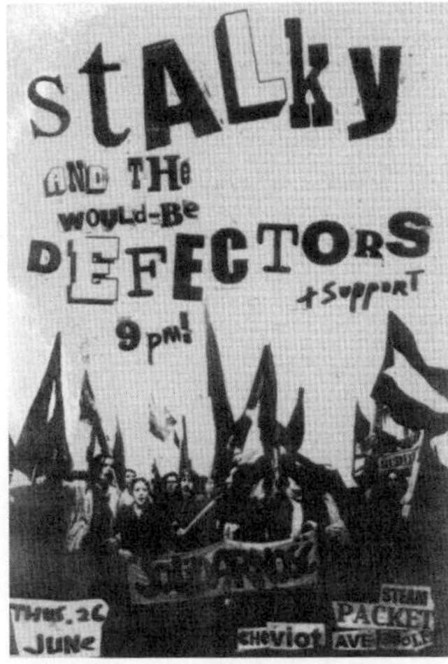

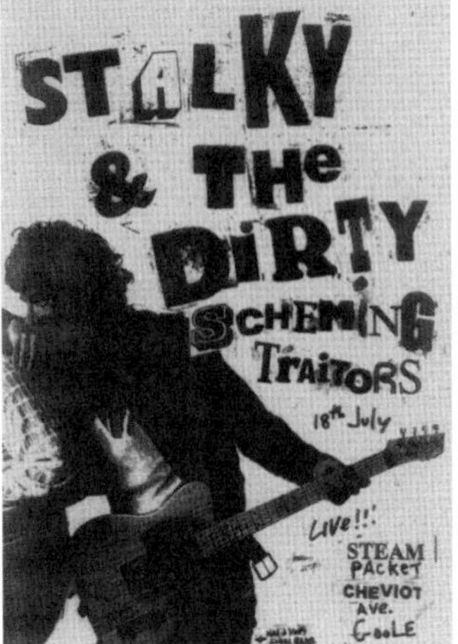

Stalky
Poster series
Scott King, 2006

CRAZY KILLER

ICH WEISS
WAS DU LETZTEN SOMMER
GESETZT HAST

25 pt

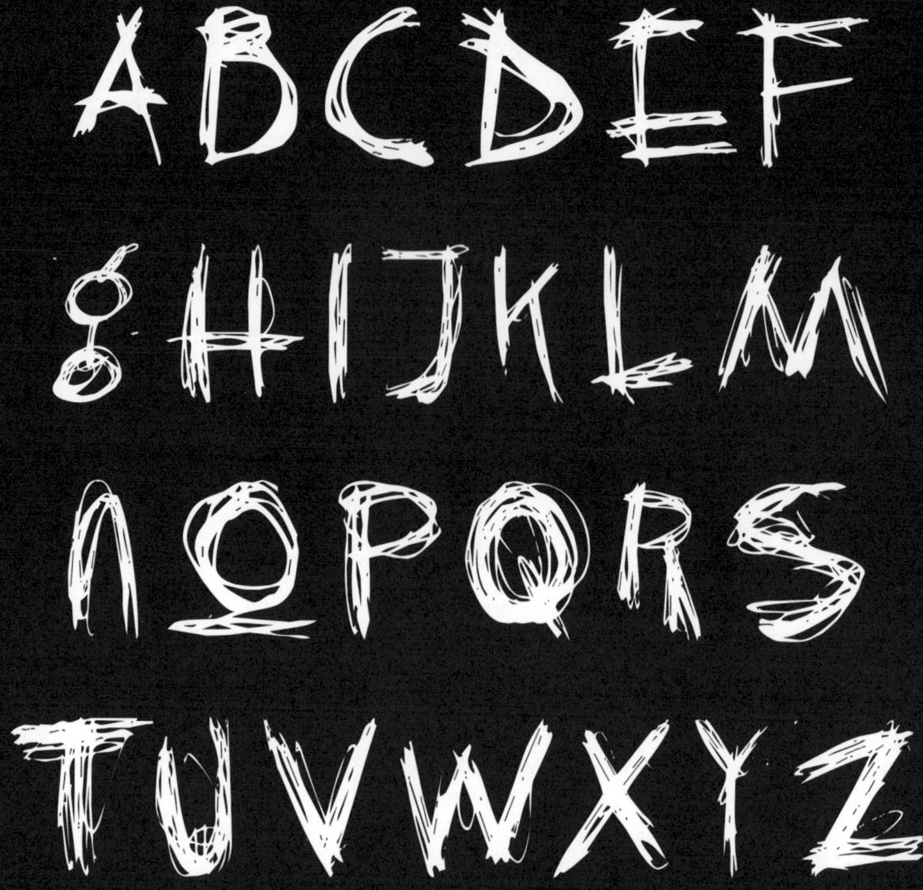

60 pt

Crazy Killer
The Font Emporium, 1998
www.dafont.com

CD

SCRATCHED OUT

120 pt

40 pt

Scratched Out
Pierredi Sciullo, 1992
www.fontfont.com

Avengers
Poster
Penelope Houston, 1977

DAUBED

115 pt

ABCDEFGHI
JKLMNOPQR
STUVWXYZ
abcdefghijklm
nopqrstuvwxyz
1234567890
(!?&ß$€ FUCK you)

42 pt

Daubed
Christoph Köckerling, 2008
www.fontsy.com

☞ CD

The Nuns
Poster, 1977

CHICKENSCRATCH AOE

125 pt

ABCDEFGHI
JKLMNOPQR
STUVWXYZ
abcdefghijklm
nopqrstuvwxyz
1234567890
(äöü!?&ß£$€@)

42 pt

ChickenScratch AOE
Brian J. Bonislawsky, 2006
www.astigmatic.com

CD

ARCADIA

Postmoderne

170 pt

A B C D E F G H I J K L M
N O P Q R S T U V W X Y Z
a b c d e f g h i j k l m
n o p q r s t u v w x y z
ä ö ü 1 2 3 4 5 6 7 8 9 0
(» ! ? & fi fl ß £ $: ; «)

56 pt

Arcadia
Neville Brody, 1990
www.linotype.com

INDUSTRIA

Eighties

160 pt

A B C D E F G H I J K L M
N O P Q R S T U V W X Y Z
a b c d e f g h i j k l m
n o p q r s t u v w x y z
ä ö ü 1 2 3 4 5 6 7 8 9 0
[» ! ? & fi fl ß £ $: ; «]

56 pt

Industria
Neville Brody, 1989
www.linotype.com

NEON LIGHTS

120 pt

ABCDEF
GHIJKL
MNOPQR
STUVW
XYZÄÖÜ
1234567890
(!?&ß£$@:;)

49 pt

Neon Lights
Allen R. Walden, 1993
www.dafont.com

CD

VARIEX

75 pt

abcdefghi
jklmnopqr
stuvwxyz
abcdefghijklm
nopqrstuvwxyz
1234567890
äöü!?&ﬁﬂß£:;

34 pt

Variex
Rudy VanderLans, Zuzana Licko, 1988
www.emigre.com

GEOMI

190 pt

ABCDEFGHI
JKLMNOPQR
STUVWXYZ
abcdefghijklm
nopqrstuvwxyz
1234567890
(äöü!?&ß$€:;)

58 pt

Geomi
Kristina Klinkmüller, 2009
www.volcano-type.de

Puma
Shop window display
C100 Purple Haze, 2008

ECHO DECO

145 pt

A B C D E F G

H I J K L M N

O P Q R S T U

V W X Y Z

1 2 3 4 5 6 7 8 9 0

(! ? & $: ;)

50 pt

Echo Deco
Rich Gast, 1999
greywolfwebworks.home.insightbb.com

☞ CD

SOPHIA

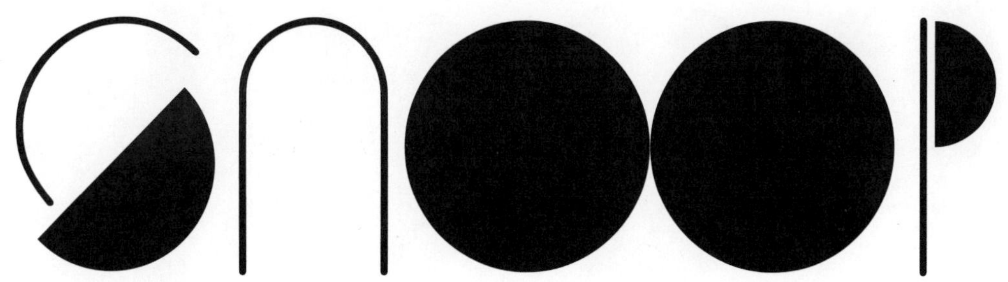

130 pt

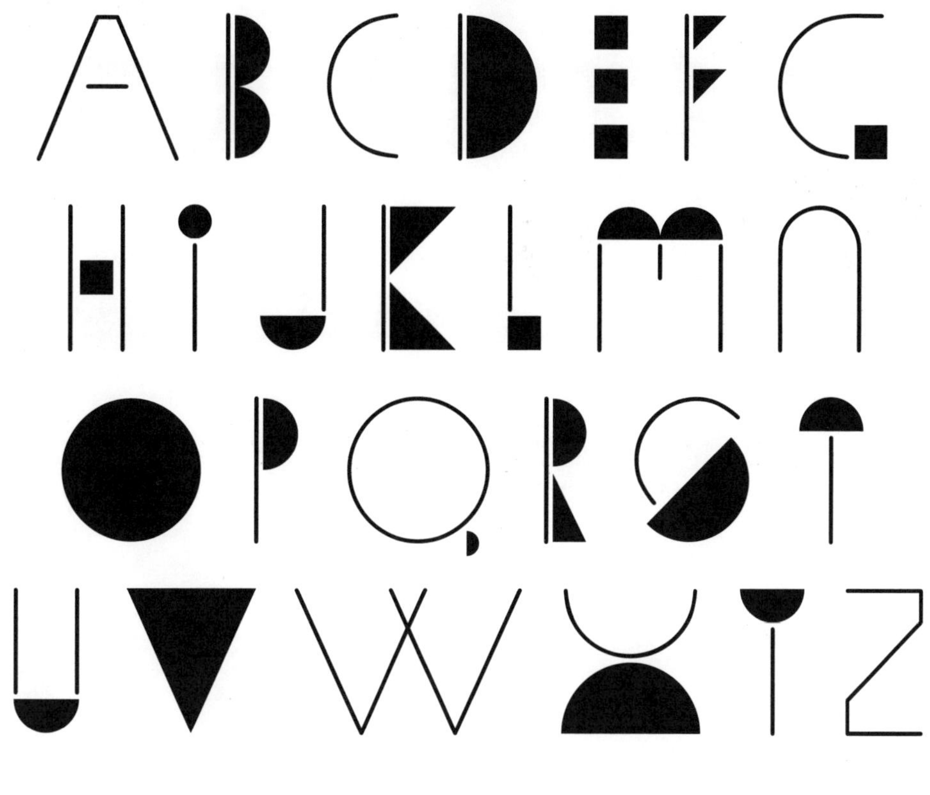

75 pt

Sophia
Jérôme Berthemet, 2008
www.dafont.com

CD

RNS BOBO DYLAN

155 pt

ABCDEFGHI

JKLMNOPQR

STUVWXYZ

1234567890

ÄÖÜ!?$

55 pt

RNS Bobo Dylan
Yorlmar Campos, 2007
www.impactolaser.com

☞ CD

Marsmobil
CD artwork
C100 Purple Haze, 2006

SINALOA

80 pt

ABCDEFG

HIJKLMNO

PQRSTUV

WXYZÄÖÜ

1234567890

(!?&£$€:;)

44 pt

Sinaloa
Rosemarie Tissi, 1974
www.linotype.com

CRACKMAN

160 pt

ABCDEFGHI

JKLMNOPQR

STUVWXYZ

1234567890

(ÄÖÜ!?&$€)

45 pt

CrackMan
Ray Larabie, 1998
www.larabiefonts.com

CD

DEKO

AKTION

80 pt

ABCD
EFGHI
JKLMN
OPQRS
TUVW
XYZ

60 pt

Deko
Ingo Zimmermann, 2006
www.ingofonts.com

CD

H&M
Postcard
Edgar Freecards, 2009

SHATTER

Videorekorder

70 pt

ABCDEFGHI
JKLMNOPQR
STUVWXYZ
abcdefghijklm
nopqrstuvwxyz
1234567890
(äöü!?&ß£$:;)

46 pt

Shatter
Vic Carless, 1973
www.linotype.com

SLIPSTREAM

WHOOOSCH!

58 pt

ABCDEFGH

IJKLMNOP

QRSTUVW

XYZÄÖÜ

1234567890

(?!&£$:;)

47 pt

Slipstream
Letraset, 1985
www.linotype.com

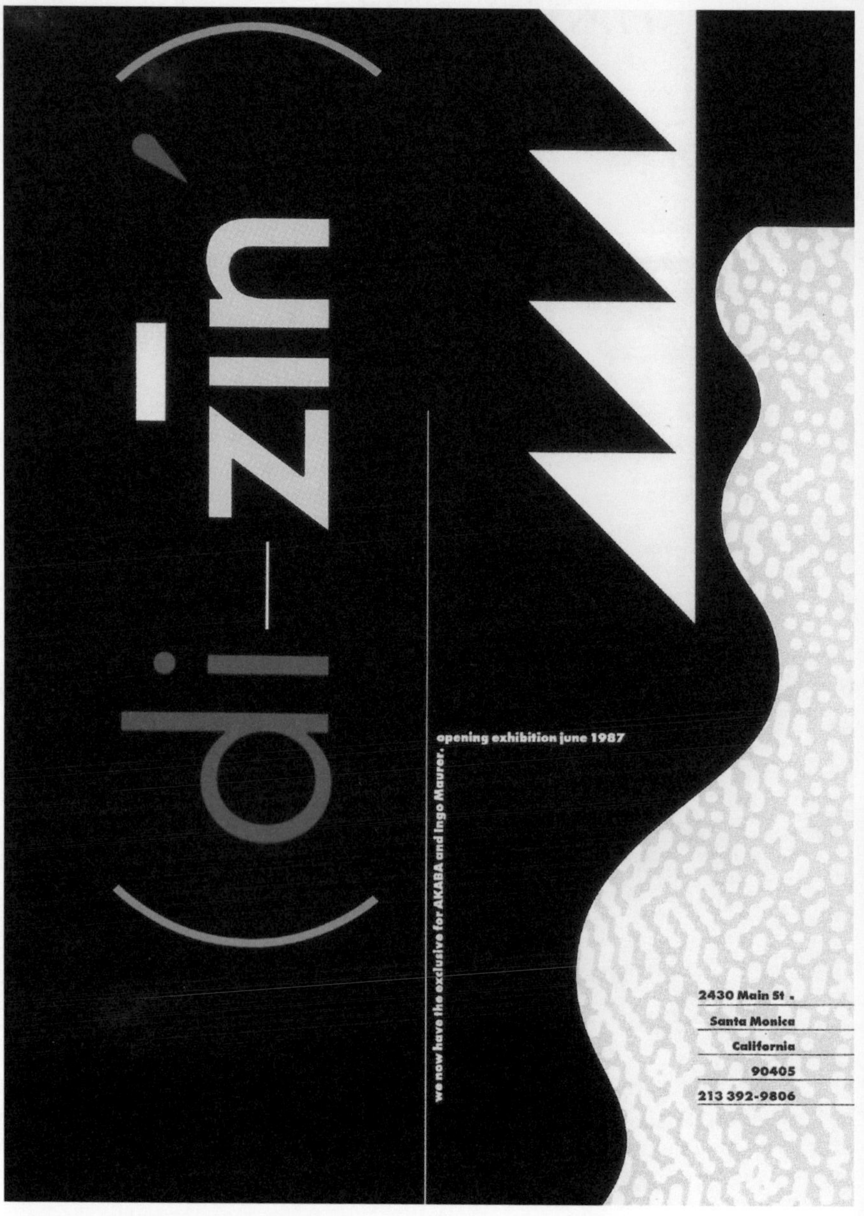

di-zin'
Poster
April Greiman, 1987

LINOTYPE BLACKWHITE

MEZZO

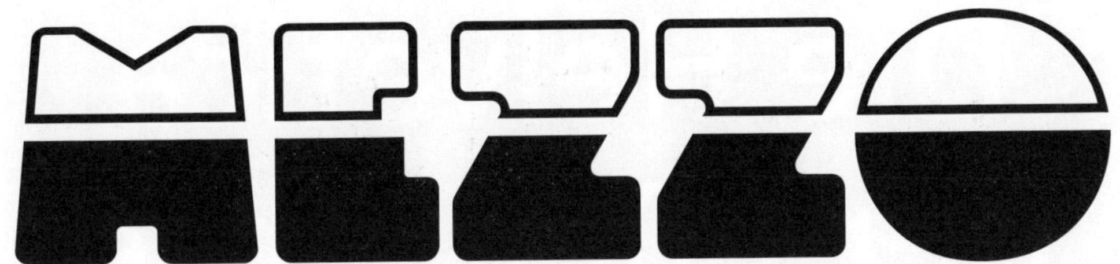

90 pt

ABCDEFG

HIJKLMNO

PQRSTUV

WXYZÄÖÜ

1234567890

(!?&£$:;)

40 pt

Linotype BlackWhite
Ferdinay Duman, 1989
www.linotype.com

FRUTIGER

Die Helvetica der 80er Jahre

50 pt

ABCDEFGHI
JKLMNOPQR
STUVWXYZ
abcdefghijklm
nopqrstuvwxyz
1234567890
(äöü!?&ß£$@:;)

41 pt

Frutiger
Adrian Frutiger, 1976
www.linotype.com

NEWS GOTHIC BT BOLD CONDENSED

Der Triumph des Corporate Design

50 pt

A B C D E F G H I
J K L M N O P Q R
S T U V W X Y Z
a b c d e f g h i j k l m
n o p q r s t u v w x y z
1 2 3 4 5 6 7 8 9 0
(ä ö ü ! ? & ß £ $ @)

40 pt

News Gothic BT Bold Condensed
Bitstream Inc., 1990
Morris Fuller Benton, 1909
www.bitstream.com

10

Bibliography

Bäumler Susanne (ed.)
Die Kunst zu werben
Munich Stadtmuseum, 1996

Baines Phil, Haslam Andrew
Type & Typography, 2nd edition
Laurence King Publishing, 2005

Böhmer Achim, Hausmann Sara
Retrodesign
Verlag Hermann Schmidt Mainz, 2009

Bank Austria (ed.)
Der optische Skandal
Kunstforum der Bank Austria, 1992

Beiersdorf AG (ed.)
Zeitdokument Werbung am Beispiel Nivea 1912–1977
Beiersdorf AG, 1977

Buchholz Kai, Wolbert Klaus
Im Designerpark
Häusser.media Verlag, 2004

Friedl Friedrich
The Univers by Adrian Frutiger
Verlag form, 1999

Hauffe Thomas
Design: A Concise History
Laurence King Publishing, 1998

Kapr Albert, Schiller Walter
Gestalt und Funktion der Typographie
VEB Fachbuchverlag, 1977

Lechner Herbert
Die Geschichte der modernen Typografie
Verlag Karl Thiemig, 1981

Lewandowsky Pina
Schnellkurs Grafik-Design
DuMont, 2006

Luidl Philipp
Die Schwabacher
Maro Verlag, 2003

Ott Nicolaus, Stein Bernard, Friedl Bernard
Typography: When, Who, Why?
Könemann, 1998

Poynor Rick
Typography Now: The Next Wave
Booth-Clibborn, 2003

Rennhofer Maria
Kunstzeitschriften der Jahrhundertwende
Christian Brandstätter Verlag & Edition, 1987

Sauthoff Daniel, Wendt Gilmar, Willberg Hans Peter
Schriften erkennen
Verlag Hermann Schmidt Mainz, 1998

Schalansky Judith
Fraktur mon Amour
Princeton Architectural Press, 2008

Schmitt Günter
Typografische Gestaltungsepochen
Arbeitsgemeinschaft für grafische Lehrmittel, 1983

Schuler Günter
Der Typo Atlas
SmartBooks, 2000

Tschichold Jan
The New Typography
University of California Press, 1995

Tschichold Jan
Schriften 1925–1974, Volume 1
Brinkmann and Bose, 1991–92

Weidemann Kurt
Typopictura – Drei Jahrzehnte werbende Typographie
Typo-Knauer, 1981

Willberg Hans Peter
Die Fraktur und der Nationalsozialismus
www.gazette.de/Archiv/Gazette-Mai2001/Willberg.html

Willberg Hans Peter
Hundert Jahre Typografische Gesellschaft München
Typografische Gesellschaft München, 1990

Willberg Hans Peter
Wegweiser Schrift
Verlag Hermann Schmidt Mainz, 2001

Copyright

Trademarks

Delphin, Frutiger, Helvetica, Kabel, Melior, Memphis, Peignot and Plak are trademarks of Linotype Corp registered in the U.S. Patent and Trademark Office and may be registered in certain other jurisdictions in the name of Linotype Corp or its licensee Linotype GmbH.

Linotype, Linotype Library, Linotype Univers, Amelia, Arnold Boecklin, Linotype BlackWhite, Choc, Linotype Dharma, Madame, Microgramma, Renner, Reporter, Salto, Saphir, Smaragd, Stymie, Tiemann and Zeppelin are trademarks of Linotype GmbH and may be registered in certain jurisdictions.

Arcadia, Auriol, Clarendon, Diskus, Eckmann, Eurostile, Industria, Insignia, Mistral, Neuland, Sistina and Umbra are trademarks of Linotype GmbH registered in the U.S. Patent and Trademark Office and may be registered in certain other jurisdictions.

Beton and Charme are Trademarks of Bauer Types. Candida, Erbar, Folio and Futura are registered Trademarks of Bauer Types.

ITC American Typewriter, Annlie, Bottleneck, Bronx, Buster, Candice, Compacta, Countdown, Data 70, Dolmen, Flamenco, Flamme, Frankfurter, Gillies Gothic,Harlow, Hawthorn, Julia Script, Octopuss, ITC Pioneer, Pump, ITC Rennie Mackintosh, ITC Ronda, Rundfunk, Shatter, Sinaloa, Slipstream, Smack, Tango, ITC Tiffany, ITC Vintage, ITC Willow and Xylo are trademarks of International Typeface Corporation and may be registered in certain jurisdictions.

ITC Avant Garde Gothic, ITC Bauhaus, ITC Benguiat, ITC Eras, Officina and ITC Souvenir are trademarks of International Typeface Corporation registered in the U.S. Patent and Trademark Office and which may be registered in certain otherjurisdictions.

Kaufmann is a registered trademark of Kingsley/ATF.

Parisian and Serpentine are trademarks of Monotype Imaging Inc. and may be registered in certain jurisdictions.

Gill Sans and Rotis are trademarks of Monotype Imaging Inc. registered in the U.S. Patent & Trademark Office and may be registered in certain jurisdictions.

Albertus, Matura, Onyx and Rockwell are trademarks of The Monotype Corporation registered in the United States Patent and Trademark Office and may be registered in certain jurisdictions.

Bernard, Binner Gothic, Broadway, Cooper Black, Gallia, Impact and Mercurius Script are trademarks of The Monotype Corporation and may be registered incertain jurisdictions.

Illustrations

El Lissitzky
Letterhead, 1925
© VG Bild-Kunst, Bonn 2009
page 230

Ludwig Hohlwein
Luftschutz!, poster, 1936
© VG Bild-Kunst, Bonn 2009
page 236

Ludwig Hohlwein
Deutsche Reichspost, poster, 1935
© VG Bild-Kunst, Bonn 2009
page 256

Eugen Max Cordier
Die Pestnot anno 1633, poster, 1949
© VG Bild-Kunst, Bonn 2009
page 344

Jacques Richez
Copaline, poster, 1971
© VG Bild-Kunst, Bonn 2009
page 440

Index of Typefaces

Index of Typefaces

J

K

L

N

R

Index of Designers

Z

Index of Foundries

Index of Foundries

Index of Foundries

Index of Illustrations

Imprint

Published in 2010 by Laurence King Publishing Ltd
363–371 City Road
London EC1V 1LR
United Kingdom
email: enquiries@laurenceking.com
www. laurenceking.com

Reprinted 2012

First published by
Verlag Hermann Schmidt Mainz
Robert-Koch-Strasse 8
55129 Mainz
Germany
email: info@typografie.de
www.typografie.de

A catalogue record for this book is available from the British Library

ISBN: 978-1-85669-681-4

Concept, text and design by Gregor Stawinski

English translation by Joel Mann

Body text typefaces: FF Quadraat, Bauer Bodoni

Cover Design: Pentagram

Printed in China